# SICK FLICKS

## VOLUME 1

### MIKE BRACKEN

NIGHTMARE FACTORY

# CONTENTS


1. Aftermath (1994) — 1

2. All Night Long (1992) — 7

3. All Night Long 2: Atrocity (1995) — 12

4. All Night Long 3: The Final Chapter (1996) — 17

5. Antropophagus (1980) — 21

6. August Underground (2002) — 26

7. August Underground: Mordum (2003) — 31

8. Bay of Blood (1971) — 36

9. The Beyond (1981) — 42

10. Black Past (1989) — 48

11. Bone Sickness (2004) — 52

12. Burial Ground (1980) — 58

13. Burning Moon, The (1992) — 62

14. Cannibal Ferox (1981) — 66

15. Cannibal Holocaust (1980) — 70

16. Cat in the Brain, A (1990) — 75

17. Cradle of Fear (2001) — 79

18. Cutting Moments (1997) — 84

| | | |
|---|---|---|
| 19. | Dawn of the Dead (1979) | 88 |
| 20. | Day of the Dead (1985) | 93 |
| 21. | Dead Alive (1992) | 98 |
| 22. | Demons (1985) | 103 |
| 23. | Entrails of a Virgin (1986) | 108 |
| 24. | Evil Dead 2: Dead by Dawn | 113 |
| 25. | Evil Dead Trap (1988) | 118 |
| 26. | The Gates of Hell (1980) | 123 |
| 27. | Guinea Pig: Devil's Experiment (1985) | 129 |
| 28. | Guinea Pig: Flower of Flesh and Blood (1985) | 133 |
| 29. | Guinea Pig: Mermaid in a Manhole (1988) | 139 |
| 30. | Guts of a Beauty (1986) | 143 |
| 31. | High Tension (2003) | 147 |
| 32. | Ichi the Killer (2001) | 152 |
| 33. | Leif Jonker's Darkness (1993) | 157 |
| 34. | Maniac (1980) | 161 |
| 35. | New York Ripper (1982) | 166 |
| 36. | Nikos the Impaler (2003) | 172 |
| 37. | Pieces (1982) | 176 |
| 38. | Plaga Zombie: The Mutant Zone (2001) | 181 |
| 39. | Premutos (1997) | 185 |
| 40. | Slaughtered Vomit Dolls (2006) | 189 |
| 41. | Splatter: Naked Blood (1995) | 194 |
| 42. | Story of Ricky, The (1991) | 198 |
| 43. | Street Trash (1987) | 202 |

44. Subconscious Cruelty (1999)                206

45. Tokyo Gore Police (2009)                211

46. The Toxic Avenger (1985)                215

47. Violent Shit (1987)                219

48. Violent Shit II (1992)                223

49. Violent Shit III—Infantry of Doom (1999)                227

50. Zombie (1979)                232

More from The Horror Geek                236

Thanks                237

# Chapter One

# AFTERMATH (1994)

**Directed by Nacho Cerda**

**Barf Bag Rating:**

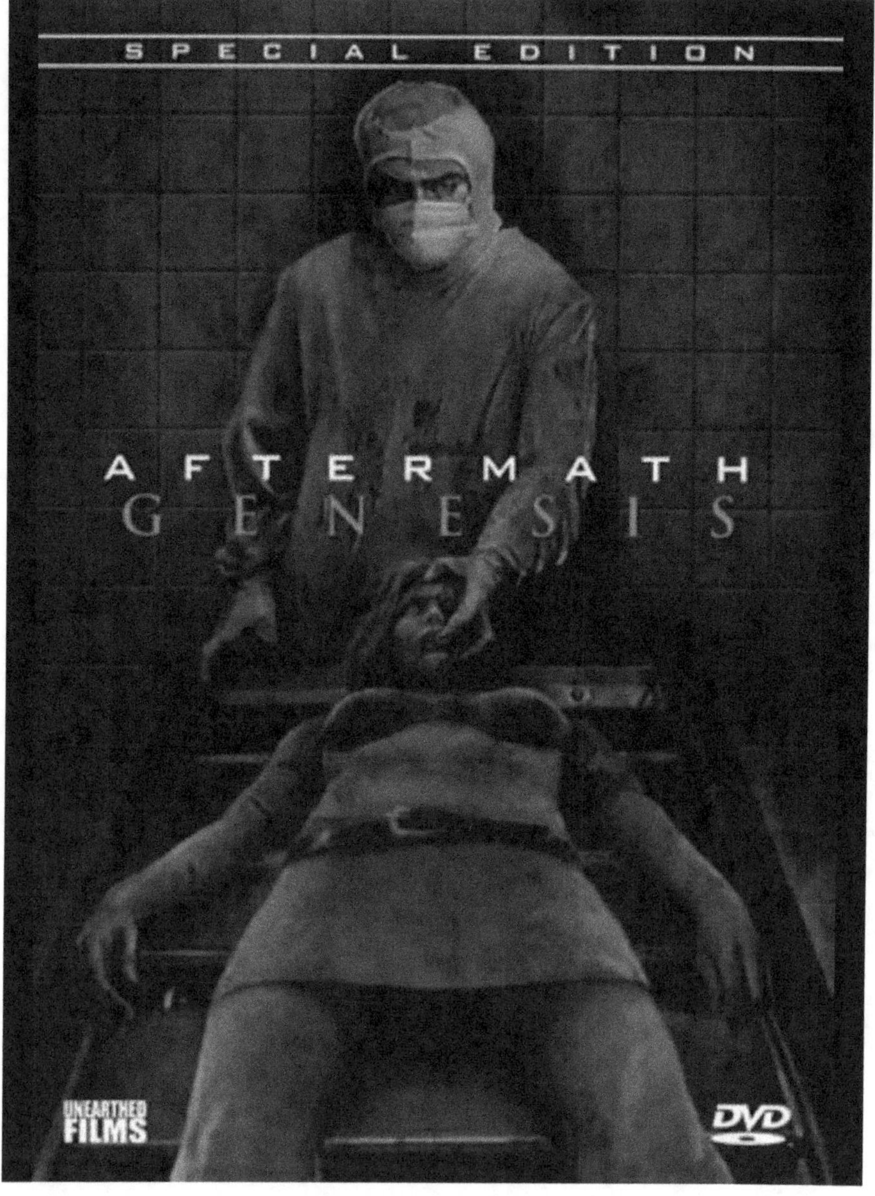
SPECIAL EDITION
AFTERMATH
GENESIS
UNEARTHED FILMS
DVD

If you were to ask the average horror or exploitation fan to name at least one film dealing with the touchy and taboo subject of necrophilia, invariably you'd get one of two responses—Jorg Buttgereit's *Nekromantik* films, or the super lame and artsy *Kissed*. And while both of these films are technically movies that deal with necrophilia, neither has anything over Nacho Cerda's powerfully disturbing 1994 short, *Aftermath*.

Cerda wrote, directed, and produced this thirty-minute exercise in extreme visceral horror and ultimately intended it to be part of a much larger film (one that was to run for over two hours). Unfortunately, financial problems necessitated truncating Cerda's vision—something that may have actually worked to the movie's advantage since few audience members could have withstood the 120+ minute visual assault the filmmaker had planned. So, instead of a longer meditation on the sexual deviancy known as necrophilia, Cerda hits us with a fast paced vignette—albeit one that packs quite a wallop from the opening shot (which is perfectly complimented by a famous Mozart Requiem) right through to the end credits.

Pep Tosar plays the lead character, a mortician working in what appears to be a local hospital. We watch as he goes about his duty, hidden away from us behind his blue surgical scrubs and a mask that covers roughly half his face. His "patients" are splayed out on the table before him, and we watch as he performs some incredibly realistic autopsies. Clothes are cut off with little regard, Y-cut incisions are made in the chest, organs are removed, weighed, and catalogued, and the cranial cavity is emptied. There's a clinical sense of detachment to these events—one that stands in stark contrast to the intimacy that is to come. Tosar is unfazed by the blood, the gore, the nudity—he's merely a man doing a job.

However, once finished with his work on the male cadavers, he discovers the battered, bloody, and ultimately dead body of Marta. I won't lie to you—there's nothing pretty about Marta in death. Yet, Tosar seems almost powerless in her presence. After checking to make sure he won't be disturbed, he cuts her clothes off and begins slowly caressing her with a surgical blade.

There's an air of ritual or fetish in these first movements—Tosar swirls the blade around her nipples, slides it casually down her sternum and over her stomach, and repeats the motion. Soon, though, things become more intense—the blade draws blood. From here, things get really wild—Tosar rapes the corpse vaginally with the scalpel, while grunting in an animalistic fashion. It's intense and savage and violent—and even though Marta can't feel a thing, the viewer can't help but feel a twinge of sorrow at the fact she must endure this final defilement.

Cerda doesn't stop there, though. Soon, Tosar is masturbating furiously to his handiwork. After that, he's photographing it. Then, he's photographing himself atop the corpse, forcing himself into her butchered openings. Once finished, he takes one last piece of Marta, an internal organ that appears to be her heart. The film finishes with Tosar's character at home, his dog eating the pureed remains of the organ. I'll leave the potential ramifications of what that might mean for you to figure out on your own.

*Aftermath* is certainly not a film for the easily disturbed or weak of stomach. Yet, while it's subject matter and graphic visual displays are disturbing, it's also one of the most beautiful films I've seen in some time. Cerda and cinematographer Christopher Baffa have created a visually arresting film that succeeds not just because of the onscreen gore, but also because of the assured camera movements, the interesting use of color, and the decision to use 35MM film as opposed to something cheaper.

It becomes readily apparent in the early going that Cerda isn't your average exploitation hack looking to make a name for himself by solely titillating his audience. Cerda and Baffa's decisions concerning how to shoot each scene have far more in common with stylistic excesses of Dario Argento than the more straightforward exploitative work of someone like Umberto Lenzi—there's clearly an aesthetic at work here, and the camera prowls along ominously in some scenes, performs the requisite Fulci-style zooms on gore effects in others, and sits distant and motionless in a few as well. Each camera movement seems carefully considered, and designed to add something to the scene in question.

The film, like Tosar, is bathed mostly in ethereal blues that seem designed to both create an oddly relaxing atmosphere, and to contrast completely with the blood and gore. The choice of color seems designed to create a visual and emotional dichotomy—the blue is serene, yet there's nothing serene going on in the blue room. At the very least, this inspires an unsettling and conflicting set of emotions in the viewer—one that gnaws at the subconscious just as surely as the gore work gnaws at your stomach.

Finally, the decision to use 35MM film stock (as opposed to the much more affordable 8 or 16MM that the *Nekromantik* films utilized) works in the movie's favor as well. The choice gives Cerda's film a much more polished and professional look overall—something that the *Nekromantik* movies were clearly missing.

Still, while the visuals and direction are superb, many folks grab this looking for some solid gore and a disturbing story—and I'm happy to report that the film gets high marks on both counts. The story is far more graphic (and, let's face it, interesting) than either of Buttgereit's pretentious films on the same subject. Cerda doesn't beat around the bush--he promises necrophilia, and he delivers—and he doesn't film it with a soft focus blurry lens, either.

The gore work was done by an FX group called DDT, and it's very impressive. The cadavers look real, as does the dissected dog shown in the very early part of the credits. Truthfully, this is some of the most impressive gore work I've seen. If you're squeamish or easily disturbed by graphic imagery, be sure to give this film a wide berth.

This review wouldn't be complete without mentioning the brilliant performance from Tosar. The actor has the very difficult task of spending 99% of the film dressed in surgical scrubs with half of his face obscured by a mask. This forces him to act mainly with his body posture, and his eyes—a difficult undertaking for any actor. Making matters even more complicated is the fact that this film doesn't feature a single line of dialogue—a few grunts and moans, but nothing in the way of spoken words. Tosar does an admirable job in such a limited role, though—we are both fearful of him and fascinated by him for the entire film...and neither

Tosar or Cerda ever give us any concrete answers about his motivations—which never allows us to formulate any kind of opinion about what drives him.

Overall, **Aftermath** is a film with a very limited audience. Its graphic take on some very disturbing subject matter is sure to offend just about everyone. And yet, it's still a surprisingly well made film. Simply put, *Aftermath* has taken necrophilia to the level of art form—I can only look forward to whatever new strange and disturbing delights Nacho Cerda has in store for us in the future.

# CHAPTER TWO

# ALL NIGHT LONG (1992)

**Directed by: Tatsuya Matsumura**

**Barf Bag Rating:**

ALL NIGHT LONG
COLLECTION
HUMAN BEINGS ARE GARBAGE

Before embarking on a career as a feature filmmaker, Katsuya Matsumura directed documentaries. It's quite possible this is what makes his ***All Night Long*** series so compellingly watchable despite the fact they're amongst some of the bleakest and most nihilistic films ever made.

As Thomas Weisser points out in his *Japanese Cinema Encyclopedia*, Matsumura's films deal with a canon referred to as "dove-style violence". In this particular field, flocks of birds have been known to single out different or weaker members of their group and peck at them until they're dead. However, rather than make a film about birds, Matsumura has taken the behavior and transmigrated it to human teenagers—with intensely disturbing results.

Shinji Saito, Kensuke Suzuki and Tetsuya Tanaka have absolutely nothing in common—at least not until all three bear witness to the savage stabbing of a young Japanese woman at a local train station. Brought together by this horrific event, the three young men form a tenuous bond despite their different social standings and goals. That each of the three youths is frustrated socially plays an increasingly vital role as the events in the film unfold. Shinji is an honor student who has no luck with women, Kensuke is the unemployed son of a well-to-do family, and Tetsuya has the simple goal of becoming an airline mechanic—a goal he can't achieve because of his poor test grades.

It's in this pent-up frustration that the three seem to find a common bond, although none of them actually realize it. Instead, our three "heroes" labor under the misguided impression that they've come together in the face of adversity—something that isn't true early on, but will become all too real later in the narrative.

Kensuke has the brilliant idea that they should have a party to celebrate their newfound friendship. He tells Shinji and Tesuya to bring their best girls for a get-together in a week. It's here that Matsumura shows us the desperate lives of these three young men.

Shinji, unable to get a date, falls in with the local bully. The bully sets him up to be humiliated by the object of his desire, but Shinji overhears the scheme. Undaunted, the young student tells the girl that he knows what she's supposed to do, and that he doesn't care—he's that desperate for a date. However, rather than have any sort of happy conclusion, Shinji becomes so panicked that he barfs on the young woman—a fate probably just as embarrassing as the one the bully had planned for him.

Kensuke, meanwhile, can't get a date either—which leads him to picking up an escort in order to maintain his macho image. Unfortunately, even that doesn't work out when the prostitute handcuffs him to a fence, pulls his pants down to his ankles, and leaves him stuck.

Tetsuya seems to be the only one with any luck—meeting up with a pretty girl who's interested in him—but as Matsumura has demonstrated throughout, life is not about happy endings in his vision of Japan. A Tokyo gang beats Tetsuya, and his date is raped and murdered.

With this final act of atrocity, even the most level-headed and seemingly well-adjusted member of the trio snaps. He gathers his two friends, scrounges up some weapons, and the three set out for revenge on the gang—a climax that comes with more than a few unexpected results.

I'm normally against writing so much plot synopsis for a film, however it's almost unavoidable with **All Night Long**. While the plot could be broken down into a simple Hollywood-style logline, it wouldn't convey the actual tone of despair that colors every frame of this film.

What's perhaps most intriguing about **All Night Long** is that it's the most "uplifting" film of the original trilogy. Here, Matsumura seems to be intent on showing that the line between being civilized and savage is a fine one, and that any of us can cross it in an instant. Later installments basically tend to equate mankind with garbage...

Typically speaking, whenever these films come up, they're invariably linked with stuff like the Japanese **Guinea Pig** films. This is an erroneous association at best. Outside of both series being born in Japan, the two sets of films have little else in common. **Guinea Pig** is a gore fan's wet dream, existing with little other purpose than to titillate an audience with its over-the-top special effects. **All Night Long** aims to say something much deeper about the nature of humanity—and while it isn't always successful, it brings a lot more to the table philosophically than any of the most popular *Guinea Pig* movies.

To say that *All Night Long* is not for everyone is a pretty major understatement. Its bleak tone, nihilistic philosophy, and entirely flawed cast of characters without much in the way of redeeming qualities can make for an unpleasant viewing experience—and one that only gets more unpleasant in subsequent films in the series. However, for those interested in looking into the abyss, they're almost essential viewing—warts and all.

# ALL NIGHT LONG 2: ATROCITY (1995)

**Directed by: Katsuya Matsumura**

**Barf Bag Rating:**

Alternate titles: *Ooru naito rongu 2: Sanji; All Night Long 2 (1995); All Night Long 2: Sanji (1995); Atrocity (1995)*

ALL NIGHT LONG
II
UNCUT EXTREME SERIES
III
CAT III
ONLY THE HARDEST FROM ASIA

If you thought that Katsuya Matsumura's 1992 film ***All Night Long*** was the darkest and most disturbing thing you'd ever seen from Japan, allow me to assure you that you haven't seen anything yet. Matsumura's follow-up, 1995's ***All Night Long 2: Atrocity*** makes the first film look lighthearted in comparison.

In this outing, Matsumura snuffs out anything that might be considered a force of good, or even viewed as remotely positive. The film (which runs a scant 68 minutes, although it's so heavy that it feels much longer) once again delves into the world of "dove-style violence". In this entry, the oddball outcast is nerdy student Shinichi (Masahi Endo). Shinichi is a weird kid—he seems to spend most of his time chatting online with a strange guy named "Good Man" or making hentai anime-styled dolls of naked women.

Shinichi owes the local youth gang money, and when he doesn't pay on time, they beat and humiliate him. While this is happening, the gang's leader (who also happens to be gay) takes a sexual interest in the young misfit. Because of this, he begins courting Shinichi—inviting him over for dinner and telling him just how much contempt he feels for his fellow gang members (he considers them beneath him). As the evening's coup de grace, Shinichi gets to meet the gangster's plaything—a young girl he's hooked on heroin, starved, keeps locked in a room, and tortures. Through the young woman, the gang leader hopes to teach Shinichi the joys of torture. He even has some success, as Shinichi attacks the girl when she laughs at him after she's performed oral sex.

Shinichi and the gang leader take the young girl to the dump, toss her in a can, and then douse her in kerosene. Only Shinichi's pleas keep the thug from lighting her on fire. His efforts go unrewarded, though—she dies anyway. This should sound vaguely familiar with anyone versed in the real life tragedy of Junko Furuta.

Even with his fledgling relationship with the gang leader, Shinichi is still on the hook for the money. He borrows cash from some friends, who in turn come to his house for a party. Unfortunately, the gang shows up too. They take everyone back to their lair and begin to rape Shinichi's female friend while beating the men and forcing them to watch. Shinichi goes psycho (in essence becoming just what his young paramour wanted him to be) and slaughters everyone in sight. In a strange final twist, as he stands amongst the carnage, he realizes that school starts the next day...

While the original *All Night Long* was released theatrically in Japan, the sequel wasn't so lucky. Despite making numerous cuts, the rating board found the tone of the entire film "unacceptable" and as such relegated it to video only.

To say that *All Night Long 2* is unrelentingly bleak isn't even worth mentioning. Many critics have compared it to Pier Paolo Pasolini's classic film *Salo: The 120 Days of Sodom*—and with good reason. Matsumura's film makes an interesting bookend when paired with Pasolini's opus when it comes to unrepentantly nihilistic and evil cinema. I don't think that *All Night Long 2* ever reaches quite the same artistic plateau as *Salo*, but they're certainly in the same thematic and aesthetic ballpark.

Matsumura once again seems intent on bludgeoning his audience with the idea that any of us can be savage—often with little or no provocation. In the first film, his anti-heroes only cross the line after the rape and murder of a young woman. Here, Shinichi doesn't need such provocation—a girl laughing at him is enough to start him down a path of no return. In fact, when it's all said and done, Shinichi winds up being even more sadistic than the gang leader—the film's antagonistic focal point up until the end of the third act.

*All Night Long* really only boasted one intense gore sequence (the murder at the train tracks), but like all good sequels, Matsumura seems to understand that he needs to up the ante this time out. Because of this, *All Night Long 2* is a much gorier film. The climax, in particular, is filled with carnage. And, even when things aren't shown onscreen, the visuals left in their aftermath are more than disturbing enough to cause viewers to fill in the blanks (for example, after the female friend is raped on the bed, Matsumura cuts to a shot of the blood and fecal-stained sheets). One standout moment is the burning face scene, which is essentially the equal of a similar shot in Lucio Fulci's *The Smuggler*.

It should be obvious that *All Night Long 2* is not for everyone. In fact, it's hardly for anyone, other than a select group of underground cinephiles who're interested in seeing what humanity may well look like at its darkest. However, if you're one of the people who fit into that narrow social strata, then this is a film you simply must see.

# CHAPTER FOUR

# ALL NIGHT LONG 3: THE FINAL CHAPTER (1996)

**Directed by: Katsuya Matsumura**

**Barf Bag Rating:**

Alternate titles: *Ooru naito rongu 3: Saishuu-shô; All night long 3: Saishûshô (1996)*

psychotic • emotional • pestilence
DVD VIDEO
Directed by
Katsuya Matsumura
with:
Yuji Kitagawa, Kanori Kadamatsu
and Tomoroh Taguchi
all night long 3
aka final atrocity
16

It seems almost hard to fathom that director Katsuya Matsumura had any contempt left for humanity after viewing the first two entries in the ***All Night Long*** series, but as ***All Night Long 3: The Final Chapter*** demonstrates, the first two films were just warm ups.

Matsumura takes his nihilist leanings to their zenith in this installment, a brutal and hopeless affair that makes the first two films seem almost positive in comparison. While previous entries in this series were certainly bleak, they always contained at least a ray of light in the form of one of the characters—something to almost disprove Matsumura's thesis that all humans are invariably garbage. ***All Night Long 3*** features no such character—it's a film adrift in a world that can only be described as amoral in the most generous of terms. No one here is without blemish—in fact, no one here actually features anything resembling a redeeming quality.

As such, viewing this installment in the series is something of an endurance test—and not one to be undertaken by the uninitiated. You almost have to wonder if this wasn't Matsumura's plan all along—make three films, with the first two hinting at his true theme, with the third an all out manifesto of his misanthropic world view. If it was, he's succeeded.

This time out, Matsumura chooses to follow Kikuo (Yuji Kitagawa), a young man who works at a local motel. Said motel is nothing more than a place for men to bring women for sex—Kikuo is part of the janitorial staff, and spends his days cleaning up in the aftermath of carnal bliss. He has something of an affinity for garbage—he collects pubic hairs, cleans up used condoms, and so forth.

This fascination with garbage eventually leads him to the trash of Hitomi Nomura (Kanori Kadomatsu, making yet another appearance in the series). Hitomi's trash isn't the leftover remnants of some idyllic tryst—it's simply sitting on a curb with other people's junk. Kikuo becomes fascinated with Hitomi through the exploration of her garbage. He knows her work schedule, her height, her weight, her bust size, her menstrual cycle, and more. Gradually, he begins to fall in love with her—keeping mementos of their imagined relationship littered about his apartment (photos, used sanitary napkins, etc.)

Unfortunately, Hitomi doesn't even notice Kikuo—and things stay as normal as they can be in a Katsuya Matsumura film. At least until Kikuo and a young man wind up staying at the hotel that Kikuo works at. It's then that all hell truly breaks loose. Kikuo's misguided lust explodes in an orgy of violence that simply must be seen to be believed.

If that weren't enough to keep audiences agitated, allow me to assure you that it doesn't even take into consideration half of the atrocities committed in this film. Kikuo is far from the only deranged individual populating this cinematic universe—instead, everyone here is twisted.

Take, for instance, the Dust-man, a fellow garbage voyeur who befriends Kikuo—his collection makes Kikuo's look pathetic. Or the hotel maid, who masturbates Kikuo while he watches other couples have sex through a heating vent. Or two school girls, who lure a man into having sex, then incapacitate him with a stun gun and rob him...or even the rest of the clean-up crew, who kidnap one of those girls, take her to a dump, rape her, then urinate on her for good measure. It's not a pretty world—something Matsumura likes to make sure his audience never forgets.

It would be easy to look at all this carnage and write off these films as simple exploitation movies designed to appeal to the lowest common denominator—and that would be wrong. While Matsumura may not hit upon any universal truths in his films, the idea that all humans are garbage, and the people are born as half-formed corpses who only truly reach their potential when they die certainly seems to have merit in some instances. In this regard, Matsumura is almost a modern day Marquis de Sade—railing against the apathy of man while reveling in it at the same time.

Like the two other films in this series, it goes without saying that ***All Night Long 3*** is not for everyone. However, gore fans who're looking for something that's both extreme and thought provoking should track down all three of Matsumura's films. Whether you agree with his worldview or not, the ideas are still ones worthy of consideration.

# CHAPTER FIVE

# ANTROPOPHAGUS (1980)

**Directed by Joe D'Amato (Aristide Massacessi)**

**Barf Bag Rating:**

Alternate titles: *Antropofago (1980); Antropophagous Beast (1980); Gomia, Terror en el Mar Egeo (1980); Grim Reaper, The (1980); Man Beast (1980); Savage Island, The (1980)*

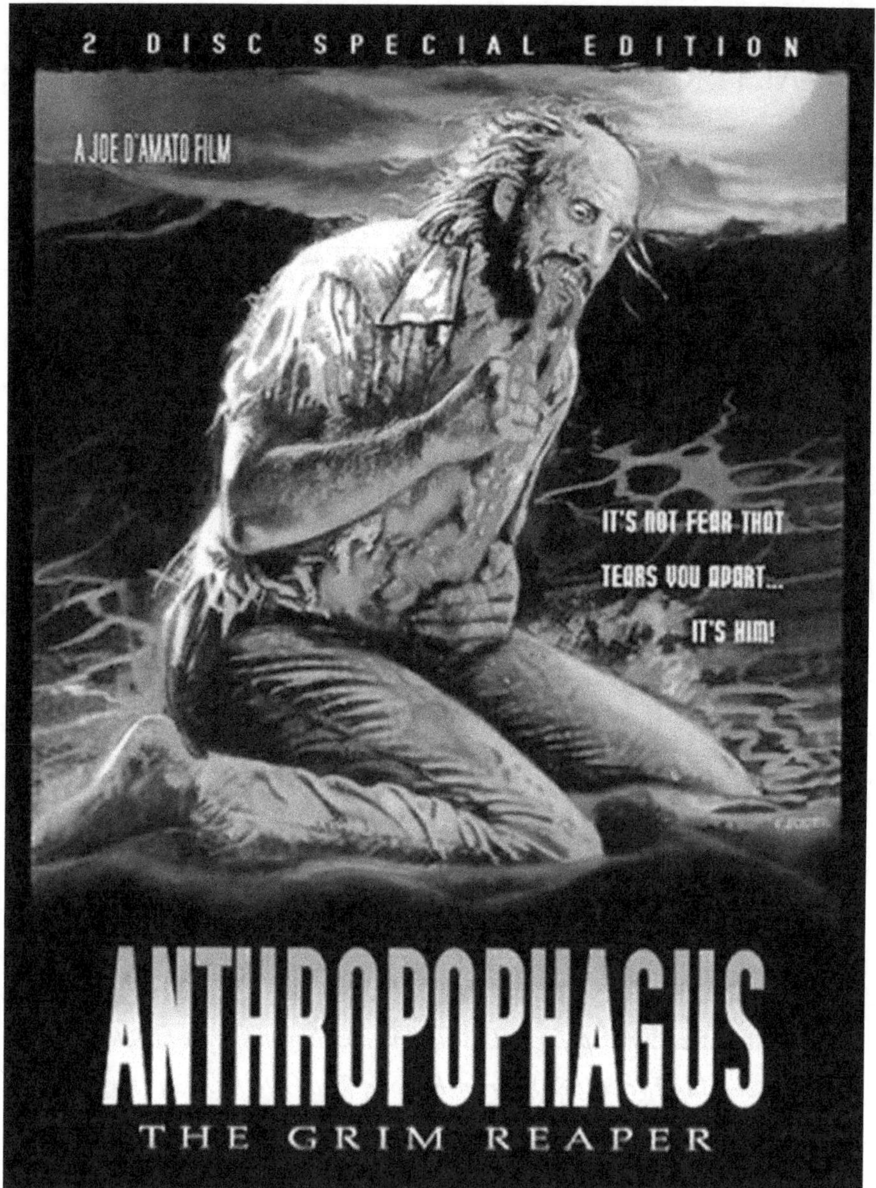
2 DISC SPECIAL EDITION
A JOE D'AMATO FILM
IT'S NOT FEAR THAT
TEARS YOU APART...
IT'S HIM!
ANTHROPOPHAGUS
THE GRIM REAPER

Joe D'Amato, aka Aristide Massacessi, is one of those cult horror directors that only hardcore fans are familiar with. With a directing career that began in the 1960s and carried on until his death in 1999 (he suffered a fatal heart attack while in Rome), D'Amato has left behind a large film legacy—everything from horror to exploitation, to *Emmanuelle* flicks (the best ones, with Laura Gemser as Emmanuelle), to hardcore porn to the sword and sandal sagas...you name it. In a way, D'Amato embodied the typical Italian exploitation director—he's not the most gifted filmmaker around, yet he made many more films than someone like a Dario Argento or Michele Soavi. And what he lacked in technical skill, D'Amato more than compensated for with a love for making films. So, now that we know a bit about Joe D'Amato the man, let's talk about *Antropophagus*, one of his most famous (or infamous, depending on your perspective) films.

*Antropophagus* centers around a group of young adults who've rented a large sailboat in order to explore an archipelago. Before leaving, they pick up an additional travel partner, Julie (Tisa Farrow). Eventually our group (comprised of a pregnant woman Maggie, her husband Arnie, a doctor-in-training Alan, young stud Danny, and psychic Carol—played by *Cannibal Ferox*'s Zora Kerova) set sail for the islands.

After the obligatory scene wherein Carol does a tarot card reading, which yields troubling results, our heroes arrive at their first destination. As they come ashore, the pregnant Maggie twists her ankle and is forced to stay behind. The others set off to explore the little island, but find it completely deserted—houses are empty, the telegraph machine is broken beyond repair, and there's not a soul in sight...except for a strange woman who disappears whenever they come near her. Soon after making this discovery, they notice that their boat is sailing out to sea—with Maggie nowhere to be found.

From there, the group spends an evening in the deserted home of Julie's friends on the island. They discover the homeowner's blind daughter hiding in the basement (she slashes Danny in fear), and she tells them of "a man who smells like blood" who's wandering the town. After Danny's murdered, they set out to find Maggie, and try to escape, but instead they run into the crazed Nikos Karamanlis (George Eastman—a pseudonym for screenwriter Luigi Montefiore)—a madman with a taste for human flesh. What ensues is a fight for survival—and not everyone will live through it.

Plot-wise, ***Antropophagus*** is a bit slow. The trademarks of D'Amato's films (the gore, the sleaze, and the nudity) aren't featured here as prominently as they are in many of the director's other films. This fact has led many fans to label ***Antropophagus*** "boring". However, I find that the film is a pleasant change of pace for a director who's always demonstrated that he has no problems making films that only work on the most base and primal levels. D'Amato actually takes the time to build tension here, and creates a film that manages to do more than simply gross out the audience in the process. In the first hour, we have a total four murders—but we only see the monster once. Instead, D'Amato spends much of the first hour of the film driving home how trapped our protagonists are, and how desolate and empty this once populated island has become.

Of course, that's not to say that ***Antropophagus*** is without gore and carnage—because it's not. In fact, this is one the original "video nasties"—the movies that got the English government all in a tizzy in the early '80s about violent content in film.

There are essentially two "money" scenes in ***Antropophagus***—a scene wherein Eastman strangles a pregnant woman then yanks the unborn fetus out and eats it, and a scene where he takes a pickaxe blow to the chest, then starts eating his own intestines as he falls to the ground. FX-wise, both shots look pretty dated. However, the fetus-eating scene has become the stuff of gore legend, and is the primary reason why the film was banned in Britain. Aside from these two scenes, the film also features a nice cleaver to the head effect, and a few ripped out throats. The gore isn't spread out evenly throughout the film, but what's there at the beginning and the end is pretty good.

The cast is largely forgettable—the characters are essentially interchangeable (particularly the males). Tisa Farrow is the best actress of the bunch, but Zora Kerova also does a nice job with a small part. Eastman steals the show, though, looking like Macho Man Randy Savage with a skin disease.

D'Amato's direction is largely hit and miss. It's quite good for long stretches, then he throws in something so awful, so pointless, that you almost lose respect for what he'd achieved prior to that scene. For example, in the opening sequence, a woman swims in the water while her boyfriend listens to headphones on the beach. She spots a rowboat nearby and swims toward it. D'Amato cuts here to an underwater shot of the woman swimming across the surface of the ocean—one almost exactly like the shot of Chrissy Watkins swimming in the opening of *Jaws*. It's a great shot—and the handling of the rest of the scene is just as good. But, in a later scene, the script has Carol lock Julie in the cemetery late at night. It's pitch black out, yet whenever D'Amato cuts to a POV shot, you can see these scenes were filmed in broad daylight. So, we go from night to day and back again, all in the same scene—D'Amato didn't even try to use a filter to make it look like night—he just intercut daytime and nighttime footage. Truthfully, it looks pretty inept.

Despite what its detractors say, I find ***Antropophagus*** to be an entertaining film. Sure, it lacks the hardcore gore and exploitation elements that D'Amato fans have to come to expect from the man's films, but it's nice to see the director branch out and try something different every once in awhile instead of adhering to formula—even Fulci didn't make gore films *all* the time. In truth, ***Antropophagus*** is a good starting point for the D'Amato neophyte—it's gory and representative of his body of horror films, but it's not as extreme as his movies like ***Buio Omega*** aka ***Beyond the Darkness*** or ***Porno Holocaust***. At any rate, if you're a fan of films that attempt to merge the slasher subgenre with the cannibal and zombie subgenres (Eastman does sort of look like a zombie, even though he's not one), or Italian gore in general, then ***Antropophagus*** is well worth tracking down.

# CHAPTER SIX

# AUGUST UNDERGROUND (2002)

**Directed by: Allen Peters and Fred Vogel**

**Barf Bag Rating:**

FRED VOGEL'S
AUGUST
UNDERGROUND
"THE SICKEST FILM EVER MADE?"

Two twenty-somethings armed only with a camcorder and a whole lot of bad intentions maim and murder their way across the Pennsylvania countryside in *August Underground*—a faux snuff documentary from Allen Peters and Fred Vogel that may well be one of the most intense, unpleasant, and nihilistic film experiences ever captured on a camera.

To call *August Underground* unpleasant doesn't begin to do it justice. This isn't a kick to the balls of mainstream horror cinema—it's a claw hammer beatdown that pummels conformity until it's nothing more than so much grue and body fluid. I'm as jaded as they come, but Fred Vogel and Allen Peters managed to shock even me—and they get my complete respect for that. This is the real deal—as close to a genuine snuff film as any of us are ever going to see...and just as horrific as the real thing would almost assuredly look.

Hailed as an American answer to the Japanese *Guinea Pig* films, *August Underground* manages to outdo its inspiration at nearly every turn. While the most gruesome of the *Guinea Pig* entries were fascinated by extreme gore, they lacked subtlety. It may come as a shock to call something as twisted and utterly depraved as *August Underground* subtle, but hear me out. There's a nuance to the filmmaking on display here that was never present in the *Guinea Pig* films. *Guinea Pig* was all about the gross-out, and while *August Underground* has no shortage of moments that will make the average viewer toss his lunch—the horror of the film isn't just physical. *August Underground* keeps some of its most disturbing moments off camera and becomes as much a beating to the audience's psyche as their gag reflex. Quite simply, there is no hope here—no happy ending, no escape, no cops who bust in and rescue the victims...it is nothing more than 70-minutes of suffering, despair, and ultimately, hopelessness.

Because of this, it's hard to view *August Underground* as "entertainment"—particularly when Vogel and Peters have gone above and beyond in their efforts to make the film play as real (any gore fan worth his salt knows that Charlie Sheen turned a *Guinea Pig* tape over to the Feds believing it to be genuine snuff—the guys at Toe Tag Pictures should have mailed Charlie a promo copy of this—the press would have been extraordinary). Shot on DV and purposely "aged" to make the final product look like a multigenerational bootleg, featuring no opening credits, and jumping edits that seem to indicate that the unseen videographer has simply stopped the tape and restarted it somewhere else, the film looks genuine. Add in some astounding FX work (Vogel, who stars as the guy in front of the camera, was a graduate of Tom Savini's FX school) and some decent "acting" and the whole thing plays as so close to real that it would assuredly fool less than savvy film viewers. In fact, the only time that film shows itself to be just a movie is in the scene where Vogel punches a hitchhiker in the face repeatedly—the punches are obviously not landing.

While it may not be entertainment in the traditional sense of the word, the film is a fine example of what can be done with the Digital Video medium. God knows I've sat through enough shot-on-video crap over the course of the past decade to know good filmmaking when I see it. This is it. Allen (who works the camera throughout) does a fine job of capturing the seemingly endless atrocities on display, yet he also seems to know when to pull away and focus on something seemingly unrelated. In this sense, the camera is essentially Allen's character (since we never actually see him) and tells a bit about his psychology.

Granted, these two men are complete and utter psychopaths and the film is a veritable catalogue of atrocities that man can commit against man (or in some cases, women). The duo's first "pet" is a naked young woman bound to a chair, covered in blood, who has had her nipple chopped off. Things get worse from there as the guys then dump urine on her, smear her with excrement, and force her to eat the chopped off toe of her dead male companion—and this is just in the early going. Things spiral ever more out of control as the film progresses—pushing the limits of taste (which, to be honest, were probably crossed in the first three minutes) and an audience's endurance.

One of the complaints leveled at the film is that it features some "boring" segments—the main characters take a trip to a slaughterhouse, a drug and sex session with some sleazy hookers lasts an eternity, etc. I think these things were almost assuredly intentional, though—on one hand, they add to the genuine feel of the film...this stuff would be edited out in a traditional movie—that it's not here makes it seem that much more real. Secondly, I think the longer segments of nothing happening serve to give the audience a break. ***August Underground*** doesn't push the envelope—it rips it to shreds. To keep an audience through the whole 70-minutes, there have to be a few places where people can stop, catch their breath, and reflect. Otherwise people would leave early and those who did stay would be so desensitized to what was happening that it would cease to have any kind of effect at all. In this regard, the film is pretty damn brilliant.

I'm delighted to see films like ***August Underground*** exist. Horror in America has become synonymous with gutless date movies and banal remakes. Real horror isn't pretty, shouldn't make you giggle, and in a perfect world, should come out of nowhere and smack you in the head with a bat. ***August Underground*** is horror cinema at its basest and most depraved. Poseurs need not even bother tracking this one down.

# Chapter Seven

# August Underground: Mordum (2003)

**Directed by: Killjoy, Jerami Cruise, Fred Vogel, Mike Schneider, Cristie Wiles**

**Barf Bag Rating:**

August Underground's
MORDUM

For those of you who thought ***August Underground*** was extreme, allow me to reassure you that you haven't seen anything yet. The guys at Toe Tag Pictures didn't rest on their laurels after the release of the original ***August Underground***—they went out and decided to see just how much farther they could take their nihilistic vision...and the result was ***August Underground: Mordum***.

Take everything from ***August Underground***, double it, and you have a basic idea of what's on tap for you with ***Mordum***—a film that definitely follows the sequel maxim of "more is better". Everything this time out is bigger, more offensive, and more audacious than the first film—there are now four killers, sex is part of the torture equation, and the body count has grown almost exponentially. While the original film certainly wasn't shy in its depiction of death and perversion, ***Mordum*** takes things to a whole other level—in essence, it's the geek's geekshow. It's not a pleasant film in any way (and I'm a little worried about anyone who views it in that manner) but it is a tour de force of independent splatter cinema—and it earns my undying respect for that.

Fred Vogel (the demented psycho from the original film) is back to slaughter more innocent victims, but this time he's brought along some friends. Joining Fred in his videotaped escapades are Maggot (Michael Schneider), Crusty (Cristie Wiles), and Necrophagia's own Killjoy. Together, the four serial slayers form an uneasy family dynamic that must be seen to be believed. Armed with a video camera and a seemingly endless well of depravity, this fearsome foursome brings death and dismemberment to the western Pennsylvania countryside.

Like the first film, ***Mordum*** has no real discernible plot—instead, it's a series of video postcards from the abyss penned by four monsters who're all the more shocking for their plainness. Part of what makes ***Mordum*** so terrifying is that we all know people not unlike the killers in this film—and while our friends might not have a room filled with decomposing corpses somewhere on their property, it's not that much of a stretch to imagine these sort of atrocities actually taking place—or that we ourselves could be the victims. The world of the ***August Underground*** films is a bleak, nihilistic, and ultimately terrifying place made all the more unpleasant by the fact that its existence seems so plausible. Evil is banal, and these killers are the very proof of that thesis. That this unsettling tone transcends the films and winds up affecting viewers after the movies end is a testament to just how good these young filmmakers are.

When you cut past the gore and the faux snuff stylings, when you cut right to the heart of these two films, the viewer is left with nothing other than the banality of evil. There's no grand reason for these brutal murders, no higher purpose—it exists almost entirely to highlight the fact that man (and, in this case, woman) is capable of almost unimaginable cruelty and that these acts are often perpetrated simply because they can be. It's because of this that the ***August Underground*** films are particularly alluring for those with a predilection for the darker things in life.

Of course, one could miss all that potential subtext and still get a kick out of ***Mordum***. As an example of fake snuff, it's not as good as the first entry. As a gore FX showcase, it actually trumps the first quite handily.

For the second time, the guys at Toe Tag have gone out of their way to artificially "age" the video on display. This once again gives the film a multigenerational bootleg look that is designed to add to the snuff cinema ambience. Instead of opting for the editing style of the first film (which was made to appear as though the videographer had simply stopped the tape and then restarted it) the guys use the poor tape quality as an excuse to cut. Rather than stopping and restarting the tape, the film instead goes grainy with ghost images of other stuff that was recorded before, or the picture tracking rolls, etc. In theory, it's a good idea—the actual execution just doesn't seem quite right, though.

What does seem right is the FX work courtesy of Jerami Cruise. The guys at Toe Tag have a Grand Guignol-esque passion for excess and the gore work on display is nothing short of fantastic. To catalogue every heinous act on display here would be to ruin half the fun of the film, but here are a few of the highlights: a scissor/penis castration, intestinal rape, copious vomiting on victims, maggot eating, and lots of sliced flesh. Viewers looking for extreme gore should definitely be pleased by what's on display here.

One of the biggest complaints leveled at the first two films in this series is that they're occasionally boring. In my review of ***August Underground*** I hypothesized that these stretches were mostly present by design—to give the audience an opportunity to catch their breath before moving on to the next atrocity. I think the same principle is on display in ***Mordum,*** although I think this film's level of violence and carnage is still so high that it loses some of its impact despite the pauses. The continual parade of brutality on display here will eventually desensitize its audience because it's so unrelenting. Because of this, the "filler" sequences in ***Mordum*** seem more bothersome than they did in the first outing because they generally fail to serve the purpose they were designed to fill. It's hard to imagine anyone proclaiming something extreme as these films as "boring" but in a way, they're right—some of the segments are just too long or add nothing to the already minimalistic narrative.

Despite the few minor problems, there's no denying that these films are truly something special (in a sick and twisted way, mind you). At their core, the ***August Underground*** films are an earnest attempt to take back the genre—to snatch it away from Hollywood and the spineless hacks who're making careers out of regurgitating formula, spewing forth an endless parade of lame sequels, remaking films that are already classic, and stealing stories from Asia and "Americanizing" them in the process. Fred Vogel and crew believe that horror should be raw, repulsive, and genuinely frightening—and ***August Underground: Mordum*** is a gleefully raised middle finger to the status quo of genre cinema.

# CHAPTER EIGHT

# BAY OF BLOOD (1971)

**Directed by: Mario Bava**

**Barf Bag Rating:**

Alternate titles: *Reazione a catena; Antefatto (1971); Bay of Blood, A (1972); (USA)Before the Fact-Ecology of a Crime (1971); Bloodbath (1980) (UK); Bloodbath Bay of Blood (1971); Bloodbath Bay of Death (1971); Carnage (1971); Ecologia del delitto (1971); Ecology of a Crime, The (1971); Last House on the Left Part II (1973) (USA): reissue title) New House on the Left (1971); Twitch of the Death Nerve (1971)*

INTERNATIONAL FILMS
DISTRIBUTION, S.A.
BAY OF BLOOD
UN FILM DE
MARIO BAVA
JANO.
CLAUDINE AUGER · LUIGI PISTILLI · CLAUDIO VOLONTE'
LAURA BETTI · LEOPOLDO TRIESTE · BRIGITTE SKAY

When you think about Italian horror, the conversation almost always tends to focus on filmmakers like Dario Argento, Lucio Fulci, Michele Soavi, and a few other directors who've acquired at least some success (or infamy) in the last twenty years. However, any astute Italian horror fan will also be sure to point out the work of the late, great, Mario Bava. Bava, who was not only a director, but an artist, cinematographer, and writer, is one of the most influential Italian horror filmmakers of all time (truthfully, he's only rivaled by Argento himself—whose influence has grown considerably since the 1970s). Bava was a gifted filmmaker with an eye for intriguing visuals and a penchant for experimenting with technique. His influence can be seen mainly in the films of Argento, who in turn has influenced Michele Soavi. However, equally impressive is the way he helped to define many of the conventions of the popular *giallo* subgenre and how he almost single-handedly created the slasher film with his 1971 movie ***Bay of Blood*** (a film that even predates Bob Clark's ***Black Christmas***—one of the films widely regarded as the first legitimate slasher movie).

Essentially, ***Bay of Blood*** plays as a twisted riff on Agatha Christie's ***And Then There Were None***—only in a much more violent and titillating fashion. Truthfully, you almost need a scorecard to keep up with the twisted and convoluted plot. The film features at least 13 characters, all of whom are at least somewhat seminal to the plot, and whose motivations come into play at various points throughout the narrative.

The film deals with a lovely bay in the country. Said body of water and the surrounding land is lusted after by a developer—however, when the wealthy old woman who owns the land refuses to sell, he has her killed—but, there's a hitch...her assailant is killed right after he kills the old woman. This launches an all out orgy of murder as relatives of the dead old woman knock each other off in order to gain control of the land. But, it doesn't stop there—Bava also introduces us a group of four teens that come to the bay in order to party at an abandoned house. Even though these kids have nothing to do with the land, they're all knocked off too—in some incredibly inventive ways to boot.

Bava keeps up the pace, and the pseudo-mystery for roughly two-thirds of the film before eventually giving us a climax where at least some of the motives are revealed—and then he wallops us with an ending scene so out of left field, and shot with his tongue very firmly in cheek, that sets us spinning all over again.

Generally, most Italian films of this nature aren't actually slashers, but are instead giallo films. The gialli are the name for Italian thrillers (so named because many of the films were based on thriller novels—which had yellow covers in Italy)...films that feature psychologically unbalanced killers who murder their victims in inventive ways. Basically, they're mysteries—full of red herrings, and featuring a climax where the killer is revealed and often dispatched in a gruesome fashion. However, **Bay of Blood** isn't a giallo...it's an honest to god slasher film. There's no real mystery here, since nearly everyone kills someone else at some point. Instead, Bava has invented the body count film—a movie where the plot exists only to get us from one murder sequence to the next, and the number of victims spirals ever higher.

Of course, Bava has created a slasher film that's far more stylish than almost anything created by American directors (the possible exception is John Carpenter's **Halloween**). Bava uses all of his technical tricks here to create a film that's absurd in plot and execution, but is consistently visually intriguing. We're treated to changing camera perspectives (switching from first person to third person—sometimes in the same scene), some inventive zooms and pullbacks (used much more impressively than Fulci, who generally tended to go overboard with this particular technique), a few really nice transitions (one is particularly nice—a cut from a phone being hung up in one scene to a gas pump being replaced in the next), and some fantastic rack focuses. Half the fun of the film is watching Bava use just about every directorial trick in the book to create a film that's still unique looking almost fifty years after its initial release.

Of course, the other half of the fun of watching **Bay of Blood** stems from the inventive death set-pieces Bava creates in order to dispatch his victims. It's impossible to watch this film and not see the influence (and I use that term somewhat loosely) it had on American slasher films—particularly **Friday the**

*13^(th) 1, 2, & 3*, a series that aped its setting (an isolated campground at a body of water), and several murder sequences (a machete to the face and the double impalement of two teens while having sex) from Bava's film. Still, if imitation is the sincerest form of flattery, Mario Bava should be feeling pretty good—since nearly every slasher film ever made owes something to his movie...at least in a tenuous sort of way.

Anyway, onto the gore...Simply put, this film delivers. We're treated to all kinds of carnage here—the aforementioned double impalement, a decapitation, strangulation, a hanging, shotgun death, a throat slashing, and more. Don't worry if the plot gets confusing—it doesn't matter--just relax and soon enough someone else will be getting offed in an entertaining way. Gore fans dig this movie for a reason—it's got some great carnage.

I haven't really talked about the cast in this review, not because they're not good, but because there are simply so many people in this movie that to catalogue them all would make this review even longer than it already is. This is essentially a slasher film...so the performances aren't Oscar caliber...but they're not bad either. Claudine Auger, Luigi Pistilli, Leopoldo Trieste. and Bridgitte Skay (who turns up in a really short miniskirt, goes skinny dipping, then dies) all do a nice job here—nothing spectacular, but nothing to make you out and out cringe, either.

Stelvio Cipriani provides the score, and like all Italian horror from this time period, it's odd, yet entertaining. Cipriani chooses some strange, almost light-hearted pieces for some scenes—and it's all oddly incongruous, but it generally works. Particularly entertaining is the music he chooses for the closing scene—the scene itself is twisted, but the music really drives the point home. At any rate, it's a solid score—not one you'll be humming after the movie has ended, but not one that will have you grabbing for the mute button, either.

***Bay of Blood*** has a plethora of alternate titles, including ***Ecology of a Crime, Bloodbath, Antefatto,*** and so on. Of all the alternate titles, none is more bothersome than ***Last House on the Left Part 2***—a title that the film was occasionally shown under while playing at American drive-ins during the 1970s. First, this film is *not* a sequel to Wes Craven's classic exploitation flick. Second, this isn't another one of those attempts by the Italians to cash in on the success of an American film (ala ***Zombie***)—***Bay of Blood*** was actually made and released in Italy *prior* to Craven's film...which makes it hard to be a pseudo-sequel.

If you're at all a fan of slasher cinema, then ***Bay of Blood*** is essential viewing. It's one of the earliest films in the slasher canon, and almost assuredly the most influential—meaning that even if you don't enjoy it, you're still seeing something at least semi-historical, and that had a profound impact upon the genre as a whole.

So, if you're looking for some gory slasher to watch, skip seeing ***Friday the 13<sup>th</sup>*** for the hundredth time and pick up ***Bay of Blood***—then sit back, turn off your brain, and see where ***Friday the 13<sup>th</sup>*** borrowed so many of its ideas from.

# Chapter Nine

# THE BEYOND (1981)

**Directed by: Lucio Fulci**

**Barf Bag Rating:**

Alternate titles: *Aldilà, L' (1981); And You Will Live in Terror: The Afterlife (1981); Beyond, The (1981); Seven Doors of Death (1983) (USA)*

Behind this doorway lie the terrifying and unspeakable secrets of hell.
No one who sees it lives to describe it.
And you shall live in darkness for all eternity.
Horror Maestro
Lucio Fulci's masterpiece of
fear and the unknown.
THE BEYOND
www.rollingthunderpictures.com

Roger Ebert compared the late Lucio Fulci (who passed away back in 1996) to the infamous Herschell Gordon Lewis, and I'd be inclined to agree with him. Both are directors that the average filmgoer has never heard of, both are revered in the horror community, and both had a genuine flair for the aesthetics of grue. Unlike Lewis, Fulci did manage to direct outside the genre, making several gialli, a western, some comedies, etc. Of course, he'll always be remembered as the gore auteur who brought us films like **New York Ripper**, **The Gates Of Hell**, **Zombi**, and his masterpiece, **The Beyond**.

Released in 1981, **The Beyond** is the story of Liza Merril (Catriona MacColl), a young woman who inherits an old New Orleans hotel. Merril is unaware that the hotel is built on one of the seven gateways to Hell (and I'd bet that once that little bit of info gets out, she's gonna take a real beating on the hotel's resale value). It appears that a painter/warlock named Sweik (Antoine St. John) was crucified and walled into the hotel's basement back in 1927 after trying to warn the locals about the gateway. As Liza prepares the hotel for re-opening, strange things start occurring. When Joe the plumber wanders into the basement (a laughable plot element since no one in New Orleans actually has a basement) to do some work, he unwittingly reopens the portal to Hell, bringing the dead back to Earth (isn't that how it always goes? Joe the plumber brings on Armageddon). Liza and Dr. John McCabe (David Warbeck) run around trying to make sense of the strange events using a mysterious book entitled EIBON. With the book's aid they discover the truth about the hotel and the gateway it's built on and try to save the world.

The film comes across as a more polished version of the earlier Fulci flick, **The Gates Of Hell**. This time out, all the pieces seem to fit: the direction is better, the FX are better (although, there are no scenes quite as cool as the intestine puking and drill to the head like in **The Gates of Hell**), the acting is better, and the score is better too. **Gates of Hell** looks like a practice run for this film, and Fulci gets just about everything right the second time around.

Narratively speaking, **The Beyond** is a shining example of the aesthetics of Italian horror cinema. The story here is disjointed and non-linear in many spots with events happening that don't appear to make any sort of logical sense. Many

American audiences are quick to condemn the Italian horror films because of this—citing it as a flaw, when in fact, it's simply an artistic difference. Italian horror films often eschew linear plots in order to create a nightmare on film feel for their movies. The disjointed narratives keep the audience off balance and plot only really becomes an issue when it's necessary to get characters from one set-piece to the next. For the Italians, it's always been about the mood and imagery—again, creating nightmares (which are rarely logical despite being terrifying) on film. As a technique, it stands in stark contrast to the methods of most American genre films, which are largely plot driven affairs (which is often why sequels are so awful—screenwriters and filmmakers feel a need to continually fill in the story, which tends to become increasingly more convoluted as a series progresses). Keep this in mind before viewing *The Beyond* and you're likely to enjoy it more because you're not preoccupied with making sense of it all.

Despite the improvements, the film does still possess some notable flaws. The dialogue in Dardano Sacchetti's script is laughable, with lines like "you have carte blanche, but not a blank check" guaranteed to have you talking to the screen like an episode of *MST3K*. Also amusing are some of the translations...notably a hospital with a "Do Not Entry" sign. Another unintentionally funny moment worth noting is the badly decomposed corpse hooked up to a brain monitor...if the corpse is rotting, odds are all brain function has ceased.

Perhaps the most annoying thing is David Warbeck's zombie killing at the film's climax. Warbeck has a .357 Magnum to shoot the zombies. He shoots several in the chest, but the undead just keep on coming. He then gets in some headshots that kill the zombies, which would lead any logical person to conclude they should keep aiming for the head...but not our David Warbeck. No sir, he keeps on aiming for the chest, finally running out of bullets and nearly being overrun by the walking undead. Really though, these are minor quibbles, and I only mention them because they make the movie amusing in a campy sort of way. Don't let these things put you off seeing the film—you'd be missing out.

This is some of Fulci's finest direction (right up there with his work on *The Psychic*, another very competently made film). Sure, the standard zooming close-ups of every gore effect are still there, but they're much more restrained than in a lot of his other work. The lighting is much improved over films like **The Gates of Hell**, meaning you can actually see what's happening on the screen. The edits are significantly smoother than the ones found in many of his other films, this time even showing some nice transition shots instead of the herky-jerky rough cuts that are standard in his earlier fare. All the way around, it's a nicely made piece of Italian horror cinema and the crown jewel of Fulci's filmography.

The film's performances are also surprisingly good. Warbeck is the real standout here, playing the classic horror film lead and looking like he's having a lot of fun doing it. MacColl is decent as the damsel in distress. Veronica Lazar also turns in a decent performance as Martha. Keep an eye open for Fulci himself, who has a brief, uncredited part as a librarian.

Germano Natali handles the FX duties, with Gianetto De Rossi doing some make-up work. The FX are quite impressive, featuring some nice looking zombies, a crucifixion, a German Shepherd ripping out its master's throat (a scene clearly inspired by Argento's **Suspiria**, but as you'd expect, Fulci trumps it in terms of gore), a man being whipped by chains (lifted from Fulci's own giallo **Don't Torture a Duckling**, but again, with the gore level upped here), decomposed bodies, bodies being dissolved by acid, and the infamous flesh-eating tarantulas.

And of course, it wouldn't be a Fulci gore film if it didn't highlight the director's preoccupation with eyes and ocular mayhem. Truthfully, the eye thing has become fetishistic for Fulci by this point and this film is the end all be all as far as brutal eye violence is concerned. In **The Beyond** eyes are gouged out with fingers, popped out with nails, eaten by tarantulas, and so on. If eyes are the windows to the soul, then Fulci clearly wants to obliterate the essence of many of the characters in this film.

Taking the eye fetish a step further, the film also boasts numerous shots where the actor's eyes are the only thing in frame (another Fulci visual staple), and several characters who have thick cataracts obscuring their vision. All in all, this movie is clearly the culmination of Fulci/Sacchetti's obsession with human eyes—and their destruction.

Fabio Frizzi's score is another winner, creating tension and building suspense throughout the narrative. Like most of the scores to Italian films in this time period, it sounds vaguely Goblin-esque...demonstrating just how profound an effect Claudio Simonetti's group had on their fellow score composers.

The film is available in a butchered "R" rated cut with the ***Seven Doors of Death*** title. Avoid seeing this version at all costs

Quite simply, ***The Beyond*** is a great film. It's a fine example of Italian horror cinema and the entire Euro-horror scene. It's the masterwork of a director who doesn't get nearly the respect he deserves, standing well above most of his other films and taking a place beside the finest works of directors like Argento, Soavi, and Bava. ***The Beyond*** is a classic Italian horror film and belongs in any genre fan's video collection.

# CHAPTER TEN

# BLACK PAST (1989)

**Directed by: Olaf Ittenbach**

**Barf Bag Rating:**

REGIA ED EFFETTI SPECIALI
OLAF ITTENBACH
ALEX VISANI
PRESENTA
GORE! GORE! GORE!
BLACK PAST
"BLACK PAST" UN FILM SCRITTO E DIRETTO DA OLAF ITTENBACH
CON OLAF ITTENBACH ANDREA ARBTER ANDRE STRYI SPECIAL FX OLAF ITTENBACH
UNA PRODUZIONE IMAS FILMPRODUKTION
SPASMO VIDEO
2018 - TUTTI I DIRITTI RISERVATI
ILLUSTRAZIONE GIORGIO CREDARO

German wunderkind Olaf Ittenbach's splattery debut certainly set the tone for things to come in the German shot-on-video gore market. This is roughly 90 minutes of **Evil Dead/Demons** homage culminating in a goregasm that makes both of its inspirations look almost quaint in comparison. And while the film is showing its age a bit, given the technology and budget at Ittenbach's disposal when the film was shot, **Black Past** still stands the test of time as one of the finest entries in the German gore canon.

I'd love to regale you with detailed plot analysis, but every print of this film that I've ever seen has been in German with no subtitles. This isn't really an issue though, because the language of animal guts and karo syrup is essentially universal. Ittenbach's films have never been particularly "deep"—and **Black Past** is no exception.

Broken down into its base components, the film revolves around a mirror that apparently turns people into murderous monsters. As the 1978 prologue demonstrates (wherein a man slaughters a young girl—not even three minutes into the film and we've got our first casualty) this mirror is bad news. Somehow, Tommy (Ittenbach in the starring role, sporting a mullet that would have made Jaromir Jagr proud) winds up with the mirror. Soon, his girlfriend is dead—but her severed head is still stalking his nightmares. Eventually, things culminate with Tommy morphing into a homicidal demon monster (the transformation sequence is lifted almost wholesale from Lamberto Bava's **Demons**) and the real fun begins—meaning viewers are treated to twenty or so minutes of the most over-the-top carnage and brutality ever caught by a camcorder. Olaf's reign of terror features complete body dismemberment by chainsaw, machete murders, impalement by scissors, gratuitous use of an axe, and more. Each savage kill sequence is accompanied by a symphony of screams (which makes a nice counterbalance to the whining of the power tools) and more fake blood and butcher shop scraps than should be allowed by law.

In some ways, the fact that the film isn't subtitled almost works to its advantage. Without being caught up in Ittenbach's usually banal dialogue, viewers can concentrate on what truly matters—the splatter. Because of this, **Black Past** often feels more like a genuine nightmare than a movie, a fact that works to the film's advantage at just about every turn. With only the most rudimentary understanding of the plot, viewers can sit back and soak in the atmosphere—and without telling dialogue divulging everything, some of the gore sequences are all the more shocking because they hit without warning.

If not for **Premutos**, this would arguably be Ittenbach's best film. It's more even than something like **Burning Moon** and more fully realized than films like **Legion of the Dead**. The young Ittenbach is a raw talent who's not yet fallen in love with his own delusions of grandeur (which made films like **Beyond the Limits** difficult to sit through for all the wrong reasons). He's the Vincent Van Gogh of gore—poised on the cusp of greatness, with a sharp straight razor hovering around his ear. If you can find this one, see it—and don't let the lack of subtitles turn you off.

# CHAPTER ELEVEN

# BONE SICKNESS (2004)

**Directed by: Brian Paulin**

**Barf Bag Rating:**

SPECIAL EDITION
BONE SICKNESS
SPLATTERRIFIC!
-UNCLE CREEPY
UNEARTHED FILMS
DVD

When it comes to gore cinema, there seem to be two prevailing types of film. On the one hand, you have the Dario Argento/Nacho Cerda/Peter Jackson school—a school wherein graphic gore is ever-present but it's never the sole reason for the movie's existence. On the other side of the coin, you have the Olaf Ittenbach/Andreas Schnaas gore films—low budget, shot on video (although Olaf has moved up to film these days), and featuring bucketloads of gore that take precedence over everything else--acting, story, directorial style, the whole shebang. Both schools have their charms (Argento and his contemporaries have made beautiful films packed with violence elevated to the level of art while Ittenbach and Schnaas are so gleefully over-the-top it's almost absurd), but the films of men like Argento and Jackson seem far more enduring than their lower-budget brethren. Horror fans will watch **Suspiria** a hundred times, while most will find sitting through **Premutos** more than twice an absolute chore.

American filmmaker Brian Paulin is one of the new breed of gore filmmakers—a director who's clearly been inspired by both the Argentos and Ittenbachs of the horror world and who creates micro-budgeted gore epics that are more Ittenbachian in their presentation than anything. Paulin's 2004 film **Bone Sickness** is a perfect example. The film is a splatterfest guaranteed to please the hardcore gorehound contingent if for no other reason that it contains almost as much blood and carnage as Jackson's magnum opus (**Dead Alive**), just minus the humor and professional production values.

While casual viewers will look at **Bone Sickness** (and Paulin's other feature films, including **At Dawn They Sleep**) as amateurish work made by a group of people with more drive than talent, that's not an entirely fair assessment.

Making a film, even a bad one, is a lot harder than most people realize. Making one with almost no money, purely as a labor of love, is even more impressive. This doesn't make up for all of **Bone Sickness**'s shortcomings (which we'll get to in a bit), but given the same conditions and circumstances, I doubt many people could make a film even this good. So, while **Bone Sickness** often looks a little cheap, and the acting seems on par with the average dinner theater production, at least Paulin has managed to make multiple films on his own terms. He's going to learn from these experiences—and while he may never be the next Argento, making these films will make him a better filmmaker as he moves on to other projects.

All that being said, ***Bone Sickness*** is an odd little low budget gore film that exists primarily to showcase Paulin and crew's talents for creating new ways to tear human bodies apart. The story (written by Paulin--meaning he has the same problem Ittenbach has in that he really should probably focus on directing and let an actual writer create the screenplays) focuses on Kristen (Darya Zabinski), a young wife taking care of her terminally ill husband Alex (Rich George). Alex has some unidentifiable ailment that's slowly eating him alive, but his best friend Thomas (director Paulin—writer, director, and actor...talk about a triple threat) refuses to let him go down without a fight.

Rather than carting the guy off to the Mayo Clinic or some other medical center, Thomas decides that the best way to help his friend recover is to feed him the ground up bones of various corpses. Naturally, this soon turns Alex into a flesh-eating monster and sets in motion a zombie holocaust sequence that's so gratuitous (in a good way), that it reminded me of the hell segments that ended Ittenbach's ***Burning Moon*** and ***Black Past***.

The nonsensical story isn't really important (which is driven home repeatedly by the various plot threads that just appear and disappear without any real explanation or resolution. What's really going on between Thomas and Kristen? Why are there demons in the graveyard?). What is important is the film's numerous gore effects sequences, which are the main reason ***Bone Sickness*** even exists. If you're a splatter connoisseur then the latter stages of this film are a veritable smorgasbord of body parts, carnage, blood that looks like cherry Kool-Aid, and extreme violence. At around the one-hour mark, Paulin basically has nothing left to say in the saga of Kristen and Alex, so he starts a zombie apocalypse and brings in a bunch of new characters (a SWAT team, a few commando guys, lots of zombie fodder...) and just cuts loose. Narratively, the last act of the film has almost nothing to do with what came before it (except that these "graveyard demon" guys decide to unleash the undead on the world), and the ensuing footage looks almost like a promo reel for what Paulin and his friends can do in terms of gore effects, but really, who cares? When you have people being ripped to pieces, blown up, eaten alive, and killed in some really imaginative ways you just sit back and go with the flow.

Freed from the shackles of narrative, Paulin lets it all hang out in that last act. The catalogue of atrocities on display at the end of ***Bone Sickness*** would make Gilles De Rais smile in appreciation. Eviscerations, beheadings, people blowing themselves up with hand grenades, and the now almost *de rigueur* fetus ripped from a pregnant woman's stomach (I only wish Joe D'Amato were alive to see how much ***Anthropophagus*** has influenced a whole new generation of gore auteurs). No one plunks down their greenbacks on a film like ***Bone Sickness*** for the story (which is forgettable), the acting (which is forgettable), or the directorial aesthetics (which are, again, forgettable).

No, people pay to see the gore (and maybe a few naked women, which Paulin provides in the form of Zabinski and Ruby Larocca)—and the gore is certainly not forgettable; although, there's so much of it later on that it has what I like to call the "strip club effect".

The Strip Club Effect is a phenomenon wherein men enter a club full of naked women and after 20 or so minutes have seen so many boobs that we become overwhelmed and desensitized to them...so many, in fact, that we'd actually rather watch the game on the big screen TV or, god forbid, talk to each other. The boobs almost become irrelevant to the point that they all just blend together into one giant boob or something.

The same thing can happen with gore—after so much carnage in such a short time, it all just blurs together, and it takes a really fantastic effects piece (or pair of breasts) to break us out of our catatonia. It should be noted that hardcore pervs and gorehounds seem to be at least somewhat immune to this effect. If you spend your cash on this film looking for crazy sequences of people being slaughtered in some of the most brutal ways imaginable, you'll be pretty pleased with ***Bone Sickness***—you just might have to watch it in increments to truly appreciate all the gross crap Paulin throws at you before everything is said and done.

While mainstream genre fans will never see this movie (and if they did, they'd trash it for not having the stars of their favorite WB shows in the cast, undoubtedly), hardcore gore aficionados will want to give ***Bone Sickness*** a look. It's got tons of shortcomings, but like the films of Olaf Ittenbach and Andreas Schnaas, it doesn't care—all ***Bone Sickness*** is really concerned with is grossing people out with elaborately crafted gore sequences. In this regard it's a success.

# Chapter Twelve

# BURIAL GROUND (1980)

**Directed by: Andrea Bianchi**

**Barf Bag Rating:**

Alternate titles: *Notti del terrore, Le; Burial Ground: The Nights of Terror (2002)(USA: DVD title); Night of Terror (1980)(UK); Nights of Terror (1980) (UK: cut version); Zombie 3: Le notti del terrore (1980) (Italy: video title); Zombie Dead, The (1980)(UK); Zombie Horror (1980)*

THE GATES OF HELL HAVE OPENED
BURIAL GROUND
SEVERIN

While the plot of ***Burial Ground*** can be best described as nonsensical, there's no denying that Andrea Bianchi's *fumetti* (a type of Italian comic book) inspired sex and gore fest is a deliriously fun romp through the world of camp cinema. From the opening moments when an extremely hairy "scientist" tells the newly risen dead to "stand back, I'm your friend" before they devour him, right on through to the infamous climactic scene between Mariangela Giordano and the absurd looking Peter Bark (aka Pietro Barcella), it's simply impossible to take anything in this film seriously.

A group of obnoxious socialites decide to spend the weekend at an isolated Italian villa. Unfortunately, said villa is about to be overrun by the newly risen dead. Why are the dead rising? Who knows. Bianchi and screenwriter Piero Regnoli (who also wrote the Riccardo Freda/Mario Bava classic ***I Vampiri***) are less concerned with offering an explanation for why these Etruscan corpses are coming back to life than they are in getting half the cast to cavort around naked before being killed in the most gruesome fashion imaginable.

To be honest, this is the right choice. There were no shortage of "serious" Italian zombie films spawned in the wake of Romero's ***Dawn of the Dead*** and Fulci's ***Zombi*** and part of what sets ***Burial Ground*** apart from the pack is it's zany sense of humor merged with a lot of softcore exploitation elements. Watching the incredibly odd looking Peter Bark (who was actually 25 at the time, and bears an odd resemblance to Dario Argento) trying to seduce his mother isn't something you're going to find in the average zombie film, but it's one of the calling cards of Bianchi's movie. The inclusion of sex in ***Burial Ground*** shouldn't really come as much of a shock, though—Bianchi directed more than his fare share of sex films in the years before helming this production (he also directed the classic giallo ***Strip Nude for Your Killer***).

Bianchi infuses ***Burial Ground*** with a mixture of casual sex and wanton gore that surely would have made the late Joe D'Amato proud. The zombies in this film have a hankering for human flesh, and they'll go to any means to get it—including using a scythe to decapitate a maid, donning monk robes and moving about incognito, and teaming up to batter down doors. Not since Umberto Lenzi's *Nightmare City* have I seen such an industrious group of dead people...

The humans, meanwhile (at least when they're not giving in to their carnal urges), are some of the dumbest people ever to appear in a zombie film. They run into closed rooms, fail repeatedly to destroy zombie heads, and generally decide on the stupidest course of action in any given situation. I've no doubt that many of you will find the real pleasure in *Burial Ground* lies in rooting for the zombies.

Most of the film's miniscule budget appears to have gone to Gino de Rossi, who crafted the film's FX sequences, and Rosario Prestopino, who handled the FX make-up work. Gino de Rossi is a veritable legend of Italian gore cinema, and while this film is hardly his crowning achievement, there are some good gore sequences.

The most famous of the lot is the scene wherein Peter Bark gnaws off Mariangela Giordano's left breast. Peter's come back as a zombie, but Mariangela just doesn't care, so she rips open her top and lets the kid go to town. Unfortunately, he bites off a little more than he can chew...

The film's other FX are impressive, particularly some of the zombie make-up. Quite honestly, *Burial Ground* boasts some of the coolest looking zombies in horror film history. The masks, many littered with writhing maggots, are excellent. Had he wanted to, Bianchi could have made a genuinely frightening gore flick utilizing these ghouls.

While hardly the greatest of the Italian zombie films made during the 1970s and '80s, *Burial Ground* is still a film worthy of its cult classic title. Boasting a weird mix of sex, violence, gore, and that indescribably strange Peter Bark character, this is a film that all horror fans need to check out.

# CHAPTER THIRTEEN

# BURNING MOON, THE (1992)

**Directed by: Olaf Ittenbach**

**Barf Bag Rating:**

NO MATTER WHAT YOU HAVE SEEN...
YOU HAVE NEVER SEEN ANYTHING LIKE...
THE BURNING MOON
"UNSPEAKABLE CARNAGE...
This is the most medically accurate
depiction of gore and human violence
in all of cinema history."
- Vice Magazine
UNCUT. UNCENSORED. UNCONSCIONABLE.

Whatever Olaf Ittenbach lacks as a technical filmmaker (and that's enough to be an entire book of its own) is made up for in pure enthusiasm. In terms of narrative and plot construction, most of this films suck—but the gleeful abandon with which he piles on the gore effects makes up for almost all of his shortcomings.

***The Burning Moon*** was Ittenbach's second directorial outing, coming three years after his little-seen debut, ***Black Past***. Like all Ittenbach fare, it exists almost solely as a showcase for some of the most disgustingly graphic special FX ever captured on tape (courtesy of Ittenbach himself—Olaf is something of a renaissance man). Pacing, narrative logic, good acting—all of that takes a backseat to the saucy stuff. His films may not be polished, but they sure are bloody—and that's enough for me.

To be fair, Ittenbach is a better filmmaker than compatriot Andreas Schnaas (of ***Violent Shit*** fame). Both directors have made a name for themselves in the shot-on-video German gore market—no doubt inspired by guys like Jorg Buttgereit. One thing that both Ittenbach and Schnaas have on Buttgereit is that their films are actually entertaining—which is not something I can say for most of the Buttgereit films I've sat through (which is all of them). Olaf may have issues with the aesthetics of filmmaking, but at least his films have never put me to sleep.

***The Burning Moon*** is an interesting entry in the director's oeuvre—an anthology flick featuring two tales and a framing device about a drug-addled loser reading sick bedtime stories to his little sister. The first story, *Julia's Lover*, is a straightforward psycho stalker piece. Escaped mental patient Clive Parker (nudge, nudge, wink, wink) goes on a date with the fetching Julia (Christ, it's like a Hellraiser fan-fic). When she figures out that he's an escaped psycho, she ditches him—and as payback he comes to her house and slaughters everyone he finds in the most grisly fashion possible.

While not nearly as ambitious as the film's second offering, *Julia's Lover* works because Ittenbach keeps things simple narratively. He does manage to insert one of the oddest dream sequences ever in the episode (which appears almost completely out of left field) and the pacing is terrible at various points, but it's a serviceable entry in the stalk-and-slash subgenre...and it features a great exploding head gag, which is one of the quickest ways to my black and twisted heart.

The second story, *The Purity*, is far more ambitious—and far more flawed—than *Julia's Lover*. A satanic priest murders and rapes women in the countryside before committing suicide. The locals think a bumbling farmer is the real killer, so they off him as retribution. Unfortunately for them, he comes back as a zombie and kills people...then people wind up in Hell, where things get really gory.

As far as splatter is concerned, *The Purity* is classic. The Hell sequence at the climax is an endless barrage of atrocity that must be seen to be believed. Demons use corkscrews on eyeballs, rip out guts, peel off faces, and in the coup de grace, they quarter a guy. It's truly a thing of beauty.

The shame of *The Purity* is that the gory excess of the FX sequences carries over to the rest of the plot. I don't mind when Ittenbach has no restraint while showing me disgusting images of human depravity. I do wish he'd reign himself in a bit when the story runs about 20-minutes longer than it needs to, following events and characters that are, at best, tangentially related to the rest of the story. This is, of course, a highlighting of Ittenbach's greatest flaw as an artist—he comes up with some grand ideas, but they're often ideas beyond the scope of his abilities. He needs a collaborator (preferably a writer) to cut the chaff. When he learns to overcome his weaknesses, his films could reach the next level.

Problems aside, fans looking for hardcore gore will not be disappointed. Sure, it often seems like Ittenbach came up with the Hell sequence then had to build a film around it. It's okay, though, because it's one hell of a sequence. ***The Burning Moon*** is not an example of great screenwriting or filmmaking—but as a primer on how to do shot-on-video gore and do it right, the film has few peers.

# CHAPTER FOURTEEN

# CANNIBAL FEROX (1981)

**Directed by: Umberto Lenzi**

**Barf Bag Rating:**

Alternate titles: *Make Them Die Slowly (1983) (USA); Woman From Deep River (1981) (Australia)*

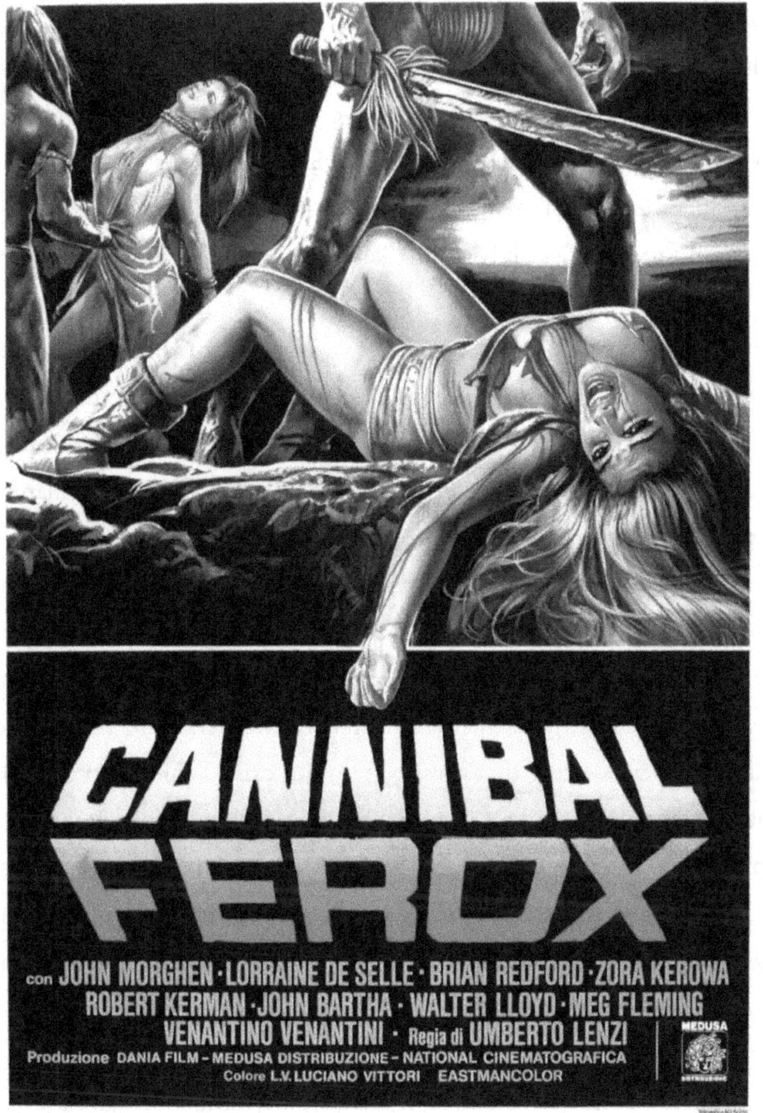
CANNIBAL FEROX
con JOHN MORGHEN · LORRAINE DE SELLE · BRIAN REDFORD · ZORA KEROWA
ROBERT KERMAN · JOHN BARTHA · WALTER LLOYD · MEG FLEMING
VENANTINO VENANTINI · Regia di UMBERTO LENZI
MEDUSA
Produzione DANIA FILM – MEDUSA DISTRIBUZIONE – NATIONAL CINEMATOGRAFICA
Colore L.V. LUCIANO VITTORI  EASTMANCOLOR

Banned in 31 countries and championed as "the most violent film ever made!", ***Cannibal Ferox*** is the stuff of exploitation legend. It's a film whispered about and lusted after by gore fans worldwide, a movie that goes out of its way to warn viewers that there are more than two dozen scenes of torture and brutality to follow and adds, "If the presentation of violent and repulsive subject matter upsets you, please do not view this film." It's a movie that got a 98 on the Joe Bob Briggs vomit meter.  Certainly a film like this would be an instant classic, right? Well, yes and no.

Attempting to ride on the coattails of 1979's classic ***Cannibal Holocaust***, ***Cannibal Ferox*** is yet another entry in the extremely popular cannibal cycle of Italian cinema. Director/writer Umberto Lenzi (who started the whole cannibal subgenre with his film ***Man From Deep River***) recreates the Amazonian setting of ***Cannibal Holocaust***, yet he drops the themes of that film, choosing instead to make a movie that exists mostly to repulse. Unfortunately, he's not totally successful.

The story deals with three anthropology students, Gloria (Lorraine De Selle), Rudy (Brian Redford), and Pat (Zora Kerova) who travel to the Amazon to research a paper asserting that cannibals do not exist. While traipsing through the jungle, they meet Mike Logan, who's played by perennial Italian cinema whipping boy Giovanni Lombardo Radice AKA John Morghen. It turns out that Logan is looking for some coke and diamonds. When he doesn't find what he's looking for, he flips out and kills some natives. This makes the natives mighty angry, and they revert back to the good old cannibal ways of old in order to make the evil white folks suffer...and boy, do they suffer.

The film also features a totally pointless subplot in which Italian cannibal film veteran Robert Kerman plays a NYC detective looking for Logan.

The film's acting is terrible, making ***Cannibal Holocaust*** look like ***Schindler's List*** in comparison. Radice is entertaining as always -- playing the Logan role with a manic glee -- but other than that, the acting is non-existent.

***Cannibal Ferox*** also suffers from some poor editing choices. The jungle scenes manage to create a real sense of unrelenting despair for the audience, yet Lenzi continually cuts away from them in order to take us back to NYC, thus destroying any of the tension the scenes had built. In one unintentionally hilarious moment, we hear the film's opening disclaimer, then watch as the movie itself opens with a shot of New York--accompanied by some super cheesy disco track. From there, we're treated to a scene with some gangsters in an apartment who curse more in the span of two minutes than Al Pacino did in the entirety of ***Scarface***. It's weird choices like this that keep the film from being as special as ***Cannibal Holocaust***.

Gino de Rossi handles the FX chores. The work alternates from superb (the castration scene) to outright laughable (the scene where the natives use a spear to cut open a man's chest...it's painfully obvious that this is a blunt spear drawing a blood trail in its wake). Again, this kind of inconsistency ultimately hurts the film because it kills any sense of tension that Lenzi's visual narrative succeeds in creating.

The occasional weak FX prop aside, the film does manage to deliver the goods in terms of gross-outs. This one's a gore/exploitation fan's wet dream, featuring eye gouging, rape, a woman hung with hooks through both of her nipples, a guy eating a great big live grub, guys impaled on sticks, gut munching, dismemberment, a lopped-off hand, a very detailed castration, and a skull hacked off so the cannibals can eat the brains right out of the head (and these last three things all happen to Radice...you gotta love this guy, he's a real-life Kenny from ***South Park***--no one dies harder in Italian cinema). Animal rights activists should skip this one, since like ***Cannibal Holocaust***, it features some real animals killed on camera — although there is a cut with all the animal cruelty footage removed.

Overall, ***Cannibal Ferox*** is a bit of a mixed bag. It suffers from an uneven pace throughout its narrative (which is odd, because Lenzi is a somewhat gifted director) and a really campy feel, yet it still manages to deliver the goods in terms of grue. If you want a harrowing jungle experience, grab ***Cannibal Holocaust***. If you want a no brains gore-fest, ***Cannibal Ferox*** is for you.

# CHAPTER FIFTEEN

# CANNIBAL HOLOCAUST (1980)

**Directed by: Ruggero Deodato**

**Barf Bag Rating:**

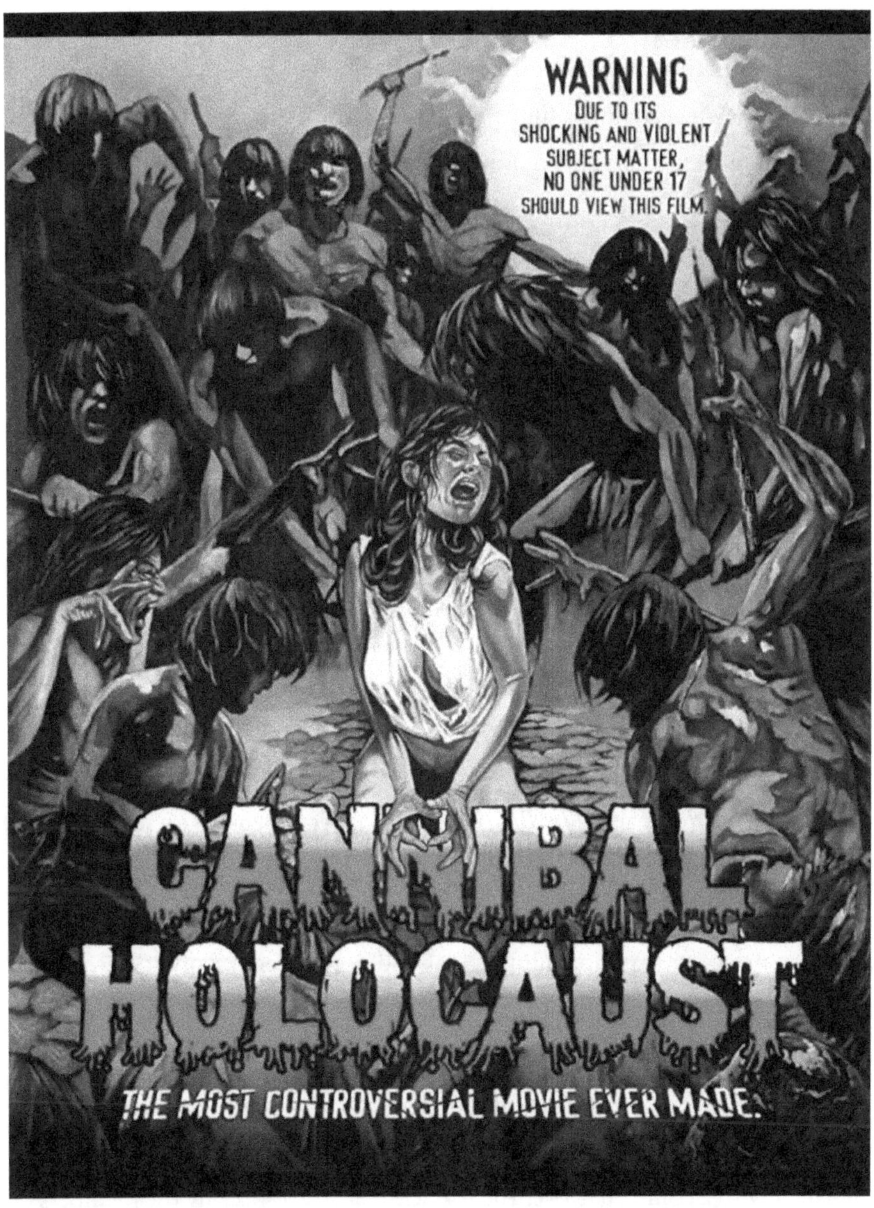
WARNING
DUE TO ITS
SHOCKING AND VIOLENT
SUBJECT MATTER,
NO ONE UNDER 17
SHOULD VIEW THIS FILM.
CANNIBAL
HOLOCAUST
THE MOST CONTROVERSIAL MOVIE EVER MADE.

One of the reasons most people can stomach horror cinema is because the films are just that—cinema. No matter how realistic, most films contain a sense of artifice that distances the viewer from the onscreen action—essentially reminding them that they're watching a film any time the action gets too intense.

Because of this, some of the most harrowing examples of horror cinema are films wherein the illusion of filmmaking—and that sense of distance and artifice—are completely sublimated. People who thought that ***The Blair Witch Project*** was real were generally more disturbed by the film than those people who were in on the faux documentary angle before entering the theater.

However, ***The Blair Witch Project*** wasn't the first film to play with an audience's perception of reality. Instead, for an even better example, one need look no further than Ruggero Deodato's classic ***Cannibal Holocaust***.

Released in 1980, ***Cannibal Holocaust*** was one of the last titles to emerge during the popular Italian cannibal cycle, yet it's regarded by many critics as the finest film in the entire subgenre. Director Ruggero Deodato manages to create a classic "chunkblower" in terms of onscreen gore, yet he also infuses the work with a sense of morality that seems strangely out of place in an Italian exploitation flick.

The film utilizes the mock documentary set-up nearly twenty years prior to ***The Last Broadcast*** and ***The Blair Witch Project***, focusing on several young mondo-style filmmakers who enter the South American jungle (referred to as the "Green Hell") to find a lost tribe of cannibals. The filmmakers never return, leading a professor (cannibal film regular and porn veteran Robert Kerman) to go in search of them roughly a year later. Kerman finds the tribe, barters for the footage, and returns to NYC--where we see what happened to the film crew.

As is to be expected in an exploitation flick, the acting is pretty bad (although not as bad as the NYC scenes in ***Cannibal Ferox***). Each thespian plays their character with a completely over the top sense of glee, especially the members of the film crew, who are the antagonists for the first half of the film. Kerman turns in a decent performance as the professor, but everyone else around him who isn't a cannibal is overacting...badly.

But, no one watches a film like ***Cannibal Holocaust*** for the performances, right? No, we watch a movie like this mainly for the gore. So, does it deliver the goods? You bet.

This is one of those films that separates hardcore horror fans from the masses. The FX work of Aldo Gasparri is impressive, especially when you stop to consider that this movie was made in the '70s, with a very limited budget, and little of today's FX technology. Scenes like the woman impaled on a pole--through her vagina and out her mouth--are incredibly realistic and much more powerful than any of today's big budget CGI horror FX. Other atrocities caught on camera include: a castration, some beatings with large hammers, gut munching, some real-life cruelty to animals (sadly, several real animals are killed on camera), and a few rapes. You're not gonna want to have a screening of this one for grandma and the kids.

Needless to say, ***Cannibal Holocaust*** has courted controversy just about everywhere. It was one the infamous "video nasties" in Britain, and it was even banned in Deodato's homeland, Italy. In fact, in an unprecedented move, Deodato had to endure an obscenity trial after being unable to convince Italian authorities that the footage was indeed staged. Deodato lost the original trial, and all prints were to be destroyed. He managed to have the ruling overturned in the early '80s.

The film is well shot, with the second half documentary footage looking extremely real. Unlike ***The Blair Witch Project***, the footage is relatively steady and shouldn't cause anyone to clutch for the Dramamine. Also worth noting is Riz Ortolani's score, which is strangely mellow, yet contrasts the onscreen carnage quite nicely.

Gianfranco Clerici's script is better than would be required in a film of this kind, managing to balance the exploitation and depravity with some moral themes. One character wonders who the real savages are in the film, and the story certainly points out that it is us. Whether it be the mondo-journalists willing to go to any extreme to get what they want on tape or the audiences who watch their efforts, it's clear that in ***Cannibal Holocaust's*** universe we are indeed the monsters. Sure, it's all dealt with in a heavy-handed way, but let's face it, nothing in this film is geared toward subtlety.

Ultimately, **Cannibal Holocaust** is a study in contrasts. Both praised and vilified, it's a powerful film that demands more than a casual viewing. It's a film so filled with images of depravity that after seeing it, you'll never be able to forget it. Fans looking for gore and nothing else would be advised to go elsewhere. Viewers looking for a cinematic experience that's powerful, visceral, and disturbing have a new title to add to their "must see" list.

# CHAPTER SIXTEEN

# CAT IN THE BRAIN, A (1990)

**Directed by: Lucio Fulci**

**Barf Bag Rating:**

Alternate titles: *Gatto nel cervello, Un; Nightmare Concert*

A CAT
in
the BRAIN
A film by LUCIO FULCI
with JEOFFREY KENNEDY - MELISSA LANG - J.L. THOMPSON - HARRISON LANG - BRETT HALSEY
and LUCIO FULCI as "Dr. Lucio Fulci"
Story and screenplay by LUCIO FULCI, GIOVANNI SIMONELLI and ANTONIO TENTORI
Director of Photography ALESSANDRO GROSSI
Editor VINCENZO TOMASSI Music FABIO FRIZZI
Produced by ANTONIO LUCIDI and LUIGI NANNERINI Directed by LUCIO FULCI
R RESTRICTED
UNDER 17 REQUIRES ACCOMPANYING
PARENT OR ADULT GUARDIAN

While Wes Craven often gets the nod for bringing self-reflexive and postmodernist tendencies to the horror genre (through his films *A New Nightmare* and the *Scream* series), more astute genre fans realize that director Lucio Fulci actually beat Craven to the punch by several years with his little seen cult classic *Cat in the Brain*. In fact, Fulci often took umbrage at the notion that Craven had done something unique by casting himself in *New Nightmare* and breaking down the fourth wall between film and reality—and in retrospect, he was probably right. Craven's film is certainly slicker in its presentation, but Fulci was clearly the first guy on the scene.

The central conceit of *Cat in the Brain* is that Fulci (playing himself) is slowly going insane from years of creating some of the most graphic depictions of gore and human depravity ever captured on film. Fulci seems obsessed with depravity while working diligently on his new feature—a film about a guy who likes to chop up women and turn them into food. Things get so bad for Fulci that he seeks out the advice of a psychiatrist (David L. Thompson)—a bad move. It seems that the doctor has some murderous urges of his own, and who better to be the patsy for his crimes than a director of horror movies? The evil doctor hypnotizes dear old Fulci and implants the suggestion that the filmmaker is responsible for committing the murders.

The film is essentially a mishmash of ideas (and scenes from other films—more on that in a bit) that never really gels into something meaningful. However, this was one of Fulci's last films, and unlike most of the output late in his career, this entry is actually pretty good. Fulci fans seem to divide almost right down the middle when it comes to discussing *Cat in the Brain*, but I'm on the side of those who find it an entertaining and underrated work.

Most of this is attributable to the fact that Fulci himself tackles the lead role. Prior to the surge in interest in Italian horror cinema (which has happened primarily in the wake of the DVD age), most of the men responsible for these odd little films were unknown to American audiences. While many fans had seen Dario Argento (who'd had several documentaries made chronicling his career), the second tier of directors like Fulci was almost entirely anonymous to all but the most hardcore spaghetti horror fanatics. So, to not only spend an entire film watching this Lucio Fulci guy in front of the camera, but to also see him in a role that was at least loosely (very loosely) autobiographical makes everything that much more interesting. Since Fulci died before the renewed interest in Italian splatter flicks (meaning we'll never get to see supplemental interviews with the master or commentary tracks expounding upon his films), this is the closest most fans will ever get to unraveling the enigma that was Fulci.

*Cat in the Brain* is a wonderfully gory affair—a real return to form for the man lovingly christened The Godfather of Gore by fans. After years of largely underwhelming and tame efforts, this was a real return to form for Fulci. *Cat* features multiple decapitations (many of them shown repeatedly for your viewing pleasure) and makes the best use of a chainsaw I've ever seen. The film is sleazy and graphic—just the things that the hardcore Fulci-phile appreciated about the maestro's work. Scenes of a woman being dismembered by a chainsaw are sure to please even the most discerning gore fan.

What's interesting is the fact that a lot of this gore and sleaze wasn't actually Fulci's. For whatever reason, *Cat in the Brain* decided to borrow liberally from roughly eight other Italian gore films (including Fulci's *Sodom's Ghost* and *Touch of Death*—for a complete list, check the appendix of Stephen Thrower's exhaustively researched *Beyond Terror: The Films of Lucio Fulci*). This cinematic splicing adds to the hazy plot progression that affects most of the film. Whether or not this bothers you is subjective—but having seen my fair share of Italian horror films, I'm pretty used to this type of thing.

Ultimately, though, *Cat in the Brain* manages to entertain more than it confounds—and that's the reason that it remains one of my favorite guilty pleasures. This isn't a great film, even by Fulci standards—but it's gory, and occasionally sleazy, and it lets the audience see a side of Fulci most of them were never exposed to. Plus, the man deserves at least some credit for bringing self-reflexivity to horror cinema years before Wes Craven managed to do it. If you love gore, or Lucio Fulci, then you owe it to yourself to at least give this one a shot.

# CHAPTER SEVENTEEN

# CRADLE OF FEAR (2001)

**Directed by: Alex Chandon**

**Barf Bag Rating:**

"Enough blood and guts to satisfy
the most terminal gorehounds...
You have been warned."
Neil Norman, Evening Standard

It's not if they die, it's how...

Pragmatic Pictures Presents
CRADLE OF FEAR
A film by Alex Chandon

STARRING DANI FILTH as THE MAN
EILEEN DALY  EMILY BOUFFANTE
STUART LAING  LOUIE BROWNSELL

DIRECTED BY ALEX CHANDON

Director Alex Chandon has been hailed as the future of British horror cinema based mostly on his work in this film. After sitting through the entire 120-minute running time of *Cradle of Fear*, I'm still trying to figure out what this really says about the state of the genre in merry old England.

On the one hand, this is a solid entry in the shot-on-video gore canon. It's bloody, suitably low-budget, and features enough carnage, death, and dismemberment to keep the average prison inmate pleased for the whole two hours. On the other, it's a bit of letdown because it seems like Chandon is a filmmaker who could be capable of so much more...if you really want to be the future of British horror, you have to do more than just phone it in, after all—and Chandon rarely seems interested in putting forth the necessary effort to take his film above the level of standard grossout cinema.

*Cradle of Fear* is an anthology film—one part the old Amicus horror anthology flicks of the days of yore, one part *Tales From the Crypt*. Unfortunately, the four stories and the framing piece that ties it all together are so poorly written that it's hard to take them seriously. Chandon (who also wrote the script) seems to labor under a belief that everyone watching the film either doesn't care about the plot and is just hanging around to see Cradle of Filth frontman Dani Filth, Emily Booth's boobs, a lot of gore effects, or is so daft that they've never experienced all of these stories told in better films and books.

The film opens with the story of Melissa—a seductive goth chick who makes the mistake of picking up Dani Filth (whose character has been imaginatively named The Man) in a nightclub.

After some wild and weird sex, Melissa starts to hallucinate—and next thing you know, she's pregnant. This isn't a normal pregnancy, though, as witnessed by the fact that the little bun in the oven tears his way out into the world while our goth heroine gives herself a home abortion. That's it—end of story. This highlights a big part of where the film fails—even *Tales From the Crypt* managed to fit some cheesy prologue into every story—a joke to tie it all together, or some reason for why the things happened. Chandon's film doesn't even bother to try (unless you count the silly wraparound story as an attempt to provide context to the tales—and even if you do, it fails pretty badly in this regard).

The second story, wherein two women rob a deaf man and murder him for his cash is at least a little better as an actual story. There's no real depth to the characters or any particular reason for them to act like they do, but at least the end of this segment has a sort of payoff.

The third story continues the upward trend, but the idea of a guy killing his friend and stealing his leg to replace his own lost limb has been done before—and done better. Naturally, the appendage takes on a mind of its own—and brings the new owner nothing but grief. Again, though, there's no real payoff to the story—it just ends.

The last tale is easily the best of the bunch (which isn't saying anything, really). Stuart Laing stars as a guy whose job involves finding websites that cross the boundaries of good taste. Unfortunately, Laing actually likes these sites—particularly one called The Sick Room wherein video voyeurs can "direct" their own snuff films. The site becomes an obsession, to the point where the man loses his job, his home, and everything else of value in his life. It doesn't matter, though, because he's found the people behind the site—and meeting them in person guarantees a whole new existence for him. The shame of it is that the ending is so badly telegraphed that it's all but obvious how the tale will turn out in the first five minutes.

Things finish up with the resolution of the wraparound story, which attempts to provide a motive for The Man and his murderous deeds. It seems that The Man kills for an asylum inmate named Kemper (more subtlety!). Kemper is the proverbial bad seed—a child killer hypnotist Satanist (talk about overkill...) who's using his demonic minion—stop me if you've heard this before--to get revenge against all the folks responsible for putting him behind bars. Naturally, dodgy cop Nielsen (Edmund Dehn—chowing down on the scenery like it's an all you can eat desert bar) has to put an end to all of this—or die trying anyway.

At two hours in length, ***Cradle of Fear*** is at least forty minutes too long. Since most of the segments have no real payoff in terms of narrative, all of them could have been trimmed significantly without actually affecting the film in a negative way. Despite this, I did enjoy the movie most of the time. Yes, it seems like a commercial for Dani Filth and his band at a lot of points, and yes the stories are bad, but unlike most gore films, there's actually some atmosphere in this one. I'm always a sucker for moody aesthetics, and that's one area where the film manages to excel. While most gore films are content to use a nonsensical story as little more than a device to get everyone to the next splatter sequence, *Cradle of Fear* tries to actually convey a mood. It doesn't always work, mind you, but it does try.

Of course, even when things are bogging down, you can rest assured that another gore segment is just around the corner. And a good splatter set-piece can make up for a lot of bad plot and acting. The quality of the effects work on display in *Cradle of Fear* is decent—it's not as low budget as Andreas Schnaas's work, nor as good as something like *Dead Alive*. What it lacks in technical proficiency, it makes up for in sheer enthusiasm. Dani Filth eats a cat's guts, a woman has her finger chopped off, heads come away from bodies, and the blood flows fast and furious. If the only thing you need in an evening's entertainment is some decent splatter, then you could do far worse than this.

I admit I'm pretty mixed on this one. The stories are so poorly developed that it's hard to like the film, yet the atmosphere, the genuine directorial talent on display, and the gore work all make a legitimate case for checking this film out. I have no idea if Alex Chandon is the future of the splatter film in England (particularly since he took a 10 year break between this film and his next directorial project), but there's enough positive stuff happening in *Cradle of Fear* that anyone with a taste for the bloodier side of cinema would be well served by checking it out.

# CHAPTER EIGHTEEN

# CUTTING MOMENTS (1997)

**Directed by: Douglas Buck**

**Barf Bag Rating:**

"...the sickest film
I've ever seen..."
-Tom Savini
FROM DUSK TIL DAWN
WINNER - MONTREAL
FANTASIA FESTIVAL
Audience Award
"...A MASTERPIECE
WHOSE DENOUEMENT
STILL HAS ME
SQUIRMING IN MY SEAT."
-Douglas E. Winter
CUTTING
MOMENTS

Running only 25-minutes and featuring like five lines of dialogue, ***Cutting Moments*** is arguably the most affecting short film I've seen since first experiencing Nacho Cerda's ***Aftermath***. Director Douglas Buck's vignette about suburbia gone horribly wrong is gut-wrenching--on a number of different levels.

The short was released as part of an anthology film entitled ***Cutting Moments*** back in 1997, but Buck's film is the real star of the show here. The other films in this anthology pale in comparison to ***Cutting Moments***—and the less said about them, the better.

Instead, viewers who stick around until the end will be treated to one of the most gruesome little shorts to emerge in years. Boasting splatter effects overseen by Tom Savini, ***Cutting Moments*** is a film guaranteed to please the gore fans.

However, dismissing the movie as just a gore film is wrong. With ***Cutting Moments*** Buck has crafted something akin to social commentary on family life, sexual frustration, and the banality of evil. Nicca Ray is Sarah, a young wife living with her sexually molested son, and the molester father (Gary Betsworth). No one ever tells the audience that this is what's happening—instead, Buck shows it through the actions of the characters. This the first and only film I've ever seen where Power Rangers dolls are used to simulate sodomy.

Sarah is repressed and depressed. The fact that her husband has more sexual interest in her son than her destroys her self-image. In a moment of anguish, after a failed attempt at seducing her husband (who can't even be bothered to look away from the baseball game on television), Sarah begins to slowly dismember herself. First she takes the steel wool to her lips, then she snips them off with a pair of scissors.

With her new look complete, she marches in front of her husband again—and the result is quite different. The two wander off to the bedroom where they mutilate each other...end of movie.

There's a veritable treasure trove of psychological interpretations for ***Cutting Moments***—and I'm not even remotely qualified to get into many of them ("Dammit Jim, I'm a film critic, not a psychiatrist!"). Rest assured though, that there's something deeper happening in this film than just an excuse to utilize some extreme gore FX. Like a good kick in the teeth, **Cutting Moments** smarts—and the pain of the viewing is one that will linger with you for a long time after the film has ended.

# CHAPTER NINETEEN

# DAWN OF THE DEAD (1979)

**Directed by: George Romero**

**Barf Bag Rating:**

Alternate titles: *Dawn of the Living Dead (1978); Zombi (1978) (Italy); Zombie: Dawn of the Dead (1978); Zombies (1978)*

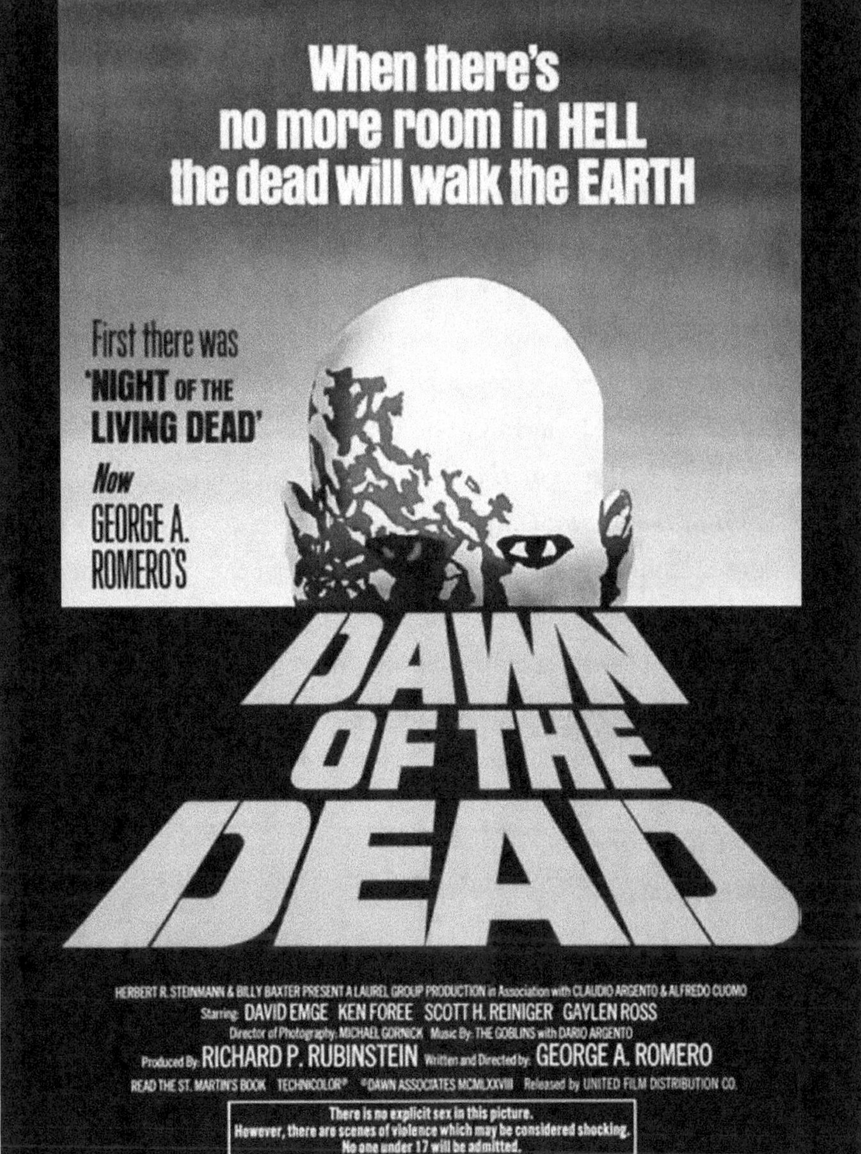
When there's
no more room in HELL
the dead will walk the EARTH

First there was
'NIGHT OF THE
LIVING DEAD'
Now
GEORGE A.
ROMERO'S

DAWN
OF THE
DEAD

HERBERT R. STEINMANN & BILLY BAXTER PRESENT A LAUREL GROUP PRODUCTION in Association with CLAUDIO ARGENTO & ALFREDO CUOMO
Starring: DAVID EMGE · KEN FOREE · SCOTT H. REINIGER · GAYLEN ROSS
Director of Photography: MICHAEL GORNICK   Music By: THE GOBLINS with DARIO ARGENTO
Produced By: RICHARD P. RUBINSTEIN   Written and Directed by: GEORGE A. ROMERO
READ THE ST. MARTIN'S BOOK   TECHNICOLOR®   ®DAWN ASSOCIATES MCMLXXVIII   Released by UNITED FILM DISTRIBUTION CO.

There is no explicit sex in this picture.
However, there are scenes of violence which may be considered shocking.
No one under 17 will be admitted.

Famous film critic Roger Ebert called George Romero's zombie classic ***Dawn of the Dead***, "an ultimate horror film!" and "a savagely satanic vision of America." And while I generally find Ebert to be fairly insightful, I can't help but feel he missed the boat here. There's no doubt that he's right when he calls ***Dawn of the Dead*** an ultimate horror film, because it is. No, where Ebert misses the mark is in his second comment—yes, ***Dawn*** is a savagely satanic vision of immense proportion, but it's a film that encompasses more than the American experience. ***Dawn*** has a decidedly bleak, almost nihilistic *worldview*—one that encompasses all of mankind, not just certain geographical regions. To see it in such confining, geocentric terms is to sell Romero's vision short.

Released in 1979, ***Dawn of the Dead*** is Romero's follow-up to his 1968 classic, ***Night of the Living Dead***. The zombie plague that began in that first film has spread, causing chaos and mass hysteria in major cities around the country. Martial law has been instituted as the powers that be bicker endlessly, trying to decide how best to deal with the epidemic. When traffic helicopter reporter Stephen (AKA Flyboy, played by David Emge) decides things are getting out of hand he steals the chopper, and along with girlfriend Frannie (Gaylen Ross), and SWAT team members Peter (Ken Foree) and Roger (Scott H. Reiniger), sets off for a better place.

The better place takes the form of a deserted shopping mall on the outskirts of Pittsburgh. While the four initially only stop in order to stock up on supplies, the allure of all the material items at their disposal entices them into staying and setting up a homestead—once they've cleared out the zombie inhabitants and secured it from outside attack.

Where ***Night of the Living Dead*** was a straight up horror film, ***Dawn*** is something a bit more intriguing. Sure, much of ***Dawn's*** first thirty minutes or so has the same bleak, unrelenting feel of the earlier film, but once our heroes arrive at their final destination, the tone changes. ***Dawn*** is something of a hybrid—a horror film with sociological impact. The film features some richly satirical moments between the explosions of violence and gore—moments that illustrate our own consumerism run amok as it raises the question: just who are the real zombies?

The shambling undead, or the four characters who become trapped by their lust for the easy life inside the mall?

And while the dead are indeed a threat, if for nothing other than their incapacitating shock value and sheer numbers, Romero makes it clear that they're a beatable threat. Mankind has the technology, the weaponry, and the ability to thwart these monsters, but we don't have the ability to work together for the common good. It's as if Romero's saying that no matter what the threat, be it nuclear holocaust or a zombie holocaust, mankind will ultimately bring about its own end through our inability to work with each other and get along—a point driven home during the film's climactic battle where Peter and Stephen face off against the biker gang led by Tom Savini.

The performances from the four main characters are all impressive, especially when one considers that they weren't famous actors. Peter and Roger in particular have a certain "everyman" quality about them that makes them both believable and likable.

The script, written by Romero and Dario Argento, is quite good as well. Unlike most genre films, this script is smart. No one does anything outlandishly stupid that leads to death. All of the risks the characters take throughout the film are for legitimate reasons—something that's rare and refreshing for a horror film.

Tom Savini provided the film's special effects work, and while the zombies themselves look fairly dated by today's standards, I'm almost inclined to believe that the design was intentional. In ***Dawn of the Dead***, the zombies look very human—only with a slightly blue-green tinge, driving home the theme that the zombies are us. The rest of the effects are excellent. Gorehounds will delight in Savini's carnage, particularly a very explosive shotgun to the head (although the one he created for William Lustig's ***Maniac*** is still the standard), a guy who's ripped apart while testing his blood pressure, and countless zombie bites scattered throughout. Also, keep an eye open for a scene in the apartment building early on...when the zombie bites into the woman's shoulder, her scream is real—it seems the zombie actor missed his mark and actually bit the actress.

***Dawn of the Dead*** has been released in countless different versions, including a theatrical cut, a European cut re-edited by Dario Argento and featuring more music from Goblin, and a 137 minute director's cut. Of the bunch, the director's cut is my favorite, and the version I recommend.

In the end, ***Dawn of the Dead*** is one of the crowning achievements in horror filmmaking. It's a visceral, yet intelligent, film that rivals the best the genre has to offer (including sacred cows like ***The Exorcist***). It's a bleak film, but one that offers a glimmer of hope at its conclusion—one signaling that while Romero feels strongly about mankind's inability to save itself, he's enough of an optimist to keep hoping we'll get it together.

***Dawn of the Dead*** is required viewing for anyone who calls themselves a horror film fan.

# CHAPTER TWENTY

# DAY OF THE DEAD (1985)

**Directed by: George Romero**

**Barf Bag Rating:**

COLLECTOR'S EDITION
GEORGE A. ROMERO'S
DAY OF THE DEAD
THE DEAD WALK!
The Darkest Day Of Horror The World Has Ever Known!

Few genre films can divide hardcore horror fans more than George Romero's 1985 zombie gut-muncher **Day of the Dead**. Its mere mention inspires heated debates from zealots and opponents alike—the kind of impassioned arguments that often occur over politics and religion. So, what is it about this little low-budget film that inspires such vehemence on the parts of its champions and detractors alike? Most likely, it's because of the film's lineage.

Romero would unleash his own special brand of the walking dead on unsuspecting audiences back in 1968, with the release of his classic **Night of the Living Dead**. **Night** was an intense and horrific little film, one that brought the zombie out of the stereotypical jungle setting and deposited him in the heart of suburbia. It's a bleak movie, filled with a strong allegorical angle that made quite a statement on 1960s America as a whole, and one that still has the power to unsettle audiences to this very day. In 1978, Romero would release his second zombie film, **Dawn of the Dead**—an undisputed masterpiece. **Dawn**'s worldview was even bleaker than **Night**'s, yet Romero chose not to totally overwhelm **Dawn**'s audience with despair by including some poignant satire about consumerism run amok. **Dawn** is a dark film, but one that you can't help but like because the characters are so interesting.

Now, jump ahead to 1985. Romero wants to make another installment in this series of films. As always, he eschews dealing with the Hollywood system—writing his own script, producing the film independently, etc. **Day of the Dead** is made, but reaction from the hardcore fans isn't as overwhelmingly positive as one might have expected. Yes, **Day** continues to build on the themes established in the first two films. Yes, it features some of the most incredibly gruesome gore effects of its time. Yes, it's certainly one of the most nihilistically bleak films ever made (up until the very end, anyway). So, why didn't it work?

**Day of the Dead** ultimately falls short for several reasons, the most glaring being the script. **Day** takes place sometime after the events in **Dawn**. America (and most likely the world) has been overrun by the shambling dead. A group of scientists and soldiers live in an underground Florida bunker—trying to figure out what makes the dead rise, and if they can be stopped. Much of the film takes place in said bunker—where the humans bicker endlessly amongst themselves as their situation becomes increasingly more dire. Unfortunately, there's not much zombie action (until the film's climax), which is what horror fans want to see in these films. And while *Night* and *Dawn* both showcased the rising tension between the humans more than the out and out zombie carnage (that was the Italian's forte), there were at least some zombie scenes to break up the monotony.

Also, the film lacks a lot of the social relevance that was so inherent in the earlier films. *Day* seems to have less depth to it—choosing to simply portray a bad situation, yet not make much of a commentary on it. This is really out of character with much of Romero's work.

To be fair, *Day* was plagued by money problems throughout its production. Romero could never get as much funding as he needed to get his complete vision on the screen—and it shows, as *Day* often looks like a half-finished film. And, to be honest, even half-finished in appearance, it's still better than 90% of the genre stuff floating around out there. A lesser director would have never pulled the film off—so Romero definitely deserves credit for that.

Another major problem lies in the performances. Romero had gotten away with using relative unknowns in both of the earlier *Dead* films, but here it just doesn't work. Lori Cardille takes the lead role as Sarah, and she's not awful, but like everyone else in the script, she's overacting. Each scene with her and Rhodes (Joe Pilato) are little more than over-the-top shouting matches. Rhodes's soldiers and Dr. Logan are even worse—hamming it up and portraying their characters as two-dimensional caricatures. Add in the stereotypical drunken Irishman and a laid back Jamaican, and well, you've got some pretty flat and clichéd characters to carry your film.

The film's final major flaw is perhaps its most egregious (at least to zombie film fans)—the inclusion of Bub. Bub is Dr. Logan's "pet" zombie—one that he's busy trying to train in order to prove that the dead can be domesticated. Bub is one of those mind-numbingly stupid creations that horror films sometimes come up with for either comic relief or as a cheap way to make an audience question their beliefs concerning who's really a monster. Honestly, it's a technique that's beneath a director of Romero's stature, and many of us are appalled by the character. Zombies are monsters—creatures that rise up with the single-minded purpose of feeding on the brains of the living—not something that can be trained like a dog. By giving them any kind of humanity, they begin to lose their power to inspire fear—which is a big mistake in a film that's supposed to terrify audiences with its portrayal of the flesh hungry undead. In short, Bub is almost the zombie equivalent of an Ewok—and that's not a good thing.

On the plus side, **Day of the Dead** is basically gore wizard Tom Savini's magnum opus as far as special effects go. As the splatterific climax ensues (which actually makes the rest of the film worth sitting through) you will see some of the most disgusting onscreen carnage ever filmed. Men are ripped in half, have their heads ripped off, and are devoured while still living. If you love gore, you'll love the final sequences of this film.

In the end, **Day of the Dead** is a good film—just not one capable of living up to its classic predecessors. Yes, it's a title that's lacking in a few key areas, filled with some B acting and flat characters, yet it still manages to frighten with it's unrelentingly bleak view of the last days of humanity. While a lot of fans complain about the upbeat ending, I almost agree with Romero's decision to go with it—the rest of **Day** is so nihilistic, so dark, that audiences needed some kind of hopeful note before leaving the theater. **Day of the Dead** is a film well worth seeing – even if I prefer **Dawn** more

# DEAD ALIVE (1992)

**Directed by: Peter Jackson**

**Barf Bag Rating:**

Alternate title: *Braindead*

Some things won't stay down...
even after they die.

DEAD ALIVE

TIMOTHY BALME  DIANA PEÑALVER  ELIZABETH MOODY  IAN WATKIN "DEAD ALIVE" PROSTHETICS DESIGN BOB McCARRON  CREATURE & GORE EFFECTS RICHARD TAYLOR  PRODUCTION DESIGN KEVIN LEONARD-JONES
MUSIC PETER DASENT  DIRECTOR OF PHOTOGRAPHY MURRAY MILNE  EDITOR JAMIE SELKIRK  SCREENPLAY STEPHEN SINCLAIR  FRANCES WALSH  PETER JACKSON
PRODUCER JIM BOOTH  DIRECTOR PETER JACKSON
A WINGNUT FILMS PRODUCTION © 1992

TRIMARK PICTURES

Due to the SHOCKING NATURE of this film, NO ONE UNDER 17 ADMITTED

The ***New York Daily News'*** Phantom of the Movies called Peter Jackson's ***Dead Alive*** "the goriest fright film of all time", and I'd be inclined to agree with him. Not since Sam Raimi' second ***Evil Dead*** film has there been a movie that so ingeniously mixes black humor and over–the-top gore. ***Dead Alive*** truly is the mother of all gore films.

Timothy Balme is Lionel, a quiet, innocent young man who lives with his widowed mother (Elizabeth Moody) in a small New Zealand town. He meets Paquita (Diana Penalver), a cute girl who's a clerk in her father's general store, and asks her if she'd like to go to the zoo with him the next day. This doesn't sit well with Lionel's mother, who follows our young lovers as they go out on their first date. As she spies on them from a distance, she has the misfortune of running into one of the zoo's more gruesome inhabitants—the dreaded Sumatran Rat Monkey (which only exists on one island in the whole world, and has allegedly evolved from the forced mating of large ship rats and the island's native monkey population). The creature bites mom, but it doesn't kill her—no, instead it turns her into a flesh eating zombie—one that Lionel doesn't have the heart to kill.

So, instead of dismembering her, or putting a bullet through her head, Lionel decides to keep her in the basement-—the only problem is, she keeps getting out and infecting more people...who also end up in Lionel's basement. Finally, after everyone thinks his mother is dead, Lionel's oafish uncle Les (Ian Watkin) shows up looking for a piece of the inheritance. When he discovers the basement's grizzly secret, he forces Lionel to sign the entire inheritance over to him, and hosts a large party at the house—a party that gives new meaning to the phrase "zombie holocaust".

With ***Dead Alive***, Peter Jackson has once again created a film that's not only disgustingly (in a good way) gory, but also undeniably hilarious. You won't know whether to laugh or puke at most of the onscreen carnage as zombies chow down on hordes of partygoers and get their just desserts during the film's 30-plus minute climax of wall-to-wall gore. Jackson's film has a wicked sense of humor that fills every aspect of ***Dead Alive***, from sight gags, situational humor, all the way through to the funny dialogue. This film is guaranteed to make you laugh and grimace...often at the same time.

As usual, Jackson's chosen to populate his film with a wide range of weird and quirky characters. There's the kung-fu priest (who in the film's most famous line tells several zombies, "I kick are for the Lord!"), the weird Nazi doctor who sells Lionel the tranquilizers to keep his basement dwellers sedated, and the zombies themselves.

Unlike your standard zombie flick, Jackson's film gives the zombies distinct personalities—which makes the proceedings even more humorous. They're a gruesome bunch, with pus-filled blisters and weird eyes, but they're actually pretty tame while Lionel keeps them tranquilized. Two even go as far as mating—producing a baby zombie in the process.

While *Dead Alive* works, for the most part, there are a few problems—most dealing with the characters' illogical actions and the lack of a definitive set of rules in relation to the zombies. Lionel takes the zombie baby out for a stroll in one outrageously funny sequence, but why? Why would he take this flesh-craving monster out of the basement? Why do some zombies die when they're dismembered, but others have body parts that keep coming back to life? Of course, it doesn't really matter. You don't watch this movie for its realistic action nor do you watch expecting it to be perfectly logical. I only point these things out because they seem like they were unnecessary narrative loose ends and that they could have easily been presented in a way that fit in with the rest of the film.

*Dead Alive* is a gory film—quite possibly the goriest film ever made. But, before you let that put you off seeing it, keep in mind that Jackson presents the blood and guts in an almost comic book style. There's so much blood, so many body parts, flying around in this film (especially at the climax, where Lionel straps on a lawn mower and cuts down hordes of the undead) that it's impossible to take it too seriously. *Dead Alive* isn't a horror film; it's a gory comedy.

Richard Taylor provided the film's creature and gore FX, and they're spectacular. From the amusingly gruesome zombies all the way through to the hideous mother monster at the film's climax, *Dead Alive* is a primer on the art of old fashioned gruesome effects work. There are loads of latex appliances, claymation, puppets, and fake blood in this film, and none of that fake looking CGI that Hollywood filmmakers have come to rely on so heavily. If gore's your bag, this film has it all—decapitations, an intestine monster, severed limbs by the hundreds, suppurating bite wounds, impalements, and more.

If you're a fan of Sam Raimi's **Evil Dead** films or any of the movies that have combined horror and comedy over the last few years, then **Dead Alive** is a title that you should seek out immediately. While it's not quite as funny as **Evil Dead 2** (it's hard to outdo Bruce Campbell), it is a very funny, extremely gross little film. And that earns high marks from me.

# CHAPTER TWENTY-TWO

# DEMONS (1985)

**Directed by: Lamberto Bava**

**Barf Bag Rating:**

Alternate title: *Demoni*

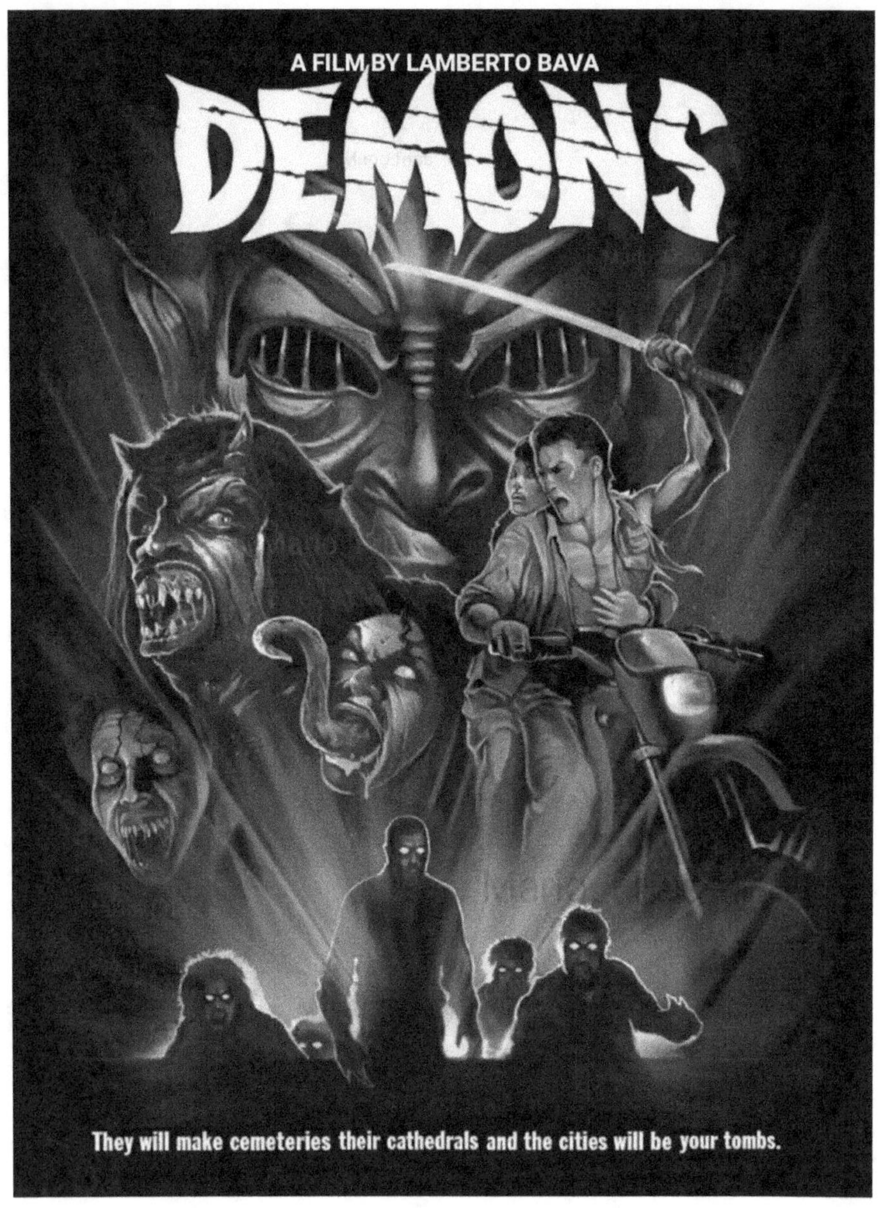

A FILM BY LAMBERTO BAVA
DEMONS
They will make cemeteries their cathedrals and the cities will be your tombs.

*"They will make cemeteries their cathedrals and the cities your tombs."*—Nost
radamus

Built around the above quote, **Demons** was the first collaboration between director Lamberto Bava (son of influential filmmaker Mario Bava) and Italian horror icon Dario Argento (who produced and co-wrote this film). It's a cult classic amongst fans of foreign gore flicks, and serves as perhaps the best starting point for those not yet initiated in the ways of Euro-horror.

**Demons** stands as a primer on the aesthetics of Italian horror, showcasing the subgenre's fascination with style over substance. The film's threadbare plot focuses on a group of diverse strangers who all receive tickets to a special screening at the newly opened Metropol theater in Berlin. After arriving, they watch a horror film about a group of teens who raid Nostradamus' tomb. The teens find a mask that causes the wearer to turn into a flesh-eating demon. It's the same mask as the one on display in the theater's lobby. As the onscreen actor (Michele Soavi) dons the mask and transforms into a monster, so too does the prostitute who tried on the one in the lobby before the film within a film started. Next thing you know, she's attacking everyone in the theater, turning them into demons too.

What ensues is a **Night of the Living Dead/Rio Bravo** style siege film. The patrons discover that the doors and windows to the theater have been mysteriously bricked up—trapping them all inside the Metropol with an ever-increasing number of monsters hungry for their flesh. The group, led by a black pimp (played by the great Bobby Rhodes, who returned in **Demons 2** as an entirely different character) and a college-aged kid (Urbano Barberini), try frantically to escape the theater and survive the night.

The script itself is full of plot holes and unanswered questions. Why is this happening? Who is behind the theater and the film? Why do some people transform faster than others? Who's the guy in the mask that gave out the tickets? Truthfully, it doesn't really matter. Bava and Argento have crafted a film that never concerns itself with logic but works anyway. Like most Italian fare, **Demons** has a definite "nightmare on celluloid" feel to it—and much like real nightmares, it doesn't feel the need to follow a linear and logical progression. If you view **Demons** in that light, it's a very effective little gore film. If you're hung up on linear plot development and sensible story twists, skip this and most of the subgenre.

Aside from the plot holes mentioned above, the film also boasts one of the greatest deus ex machina endings of modern times. With no way to get the protagonists out of the theater as the film's climax approaches, Bava decides to have a large helicopter crash through the roof, thereby creating an avenue of escape for the survivors. It's so absurd that it's actually amusing. I couldn't tell you what they were thinking when they came up with that one--it almost seems like a joke.

Bava will never be accused of being as talented as his father, but **Demons** does feature some striking visuals—which are what fans have come to expect from these kinds of films. The helicopter crash, for all of its absurdity, is actually pretty good, as are the backlit shots of hordes of demons advancing on the survivors—eyes glowing out of the darkness. Equally impressive is the long sequence near the climax where Barberini and Hovey ride through the aisles of the theater on a dirt-bike, skewering demons with a samurai sword.

The film's performances are pretty forgettable, save for Rhodes, who steals every scene he's in as the pimp. If I ever wind up in a demon-filled theater, I'd want a guy like Rhodes on my side.

Sergio Stivaletti provides the film's impressive gore effects. Viewers are treated to numerous demon bites, slashings, stabbings, bite wounds, a guy who gets his eyes popped out, demon transformations (full of exploding lesions filled with green pus), and more. Gore fans love this film for a reason—it delivers the goods in terms of onscreen carnage.

Ultimately, **Demons** stands as a film that's long on style and short on logic. Bava and company never let plot or continuity get in the way of their true goal—creating a gross and stylish movie that captures the feel of a nightmare on film. **Demons** was followed by one true sequel (**Demons 2**) and a plethora of other films all labeled with the **Demons** title in order to try and cash in (Soavi's **The Church**, Lenzi's **Black Demons**, and Bava's **The Ogre** have all been called **Demons 3**, Soavi's **The Sect** has been called **Demons 4**, and **Cemetery Man** labeled ***Demons 5***). Truthfully, it's a tenuous connection—none of these films are direct sequels, but they are good films worth checking out on their own.

***Demons*** is a solid example of Italian sensibilities when it comes to horror films—an aesthetic that differs greatly from their American counterparts. If you've never seen an Italian gore flick, ***Demons*** is a good starting point—it's accessible, but it's not the finest the subgenre has to offer. Still, it gets a high recommendation from me. Check it out.

# CHAPTER TWENTY-THREE

# ENTRAILS OF A VIRGIN (1986)

**Directed by: Kazuo "Gaira" Komizu**

**Barf Bag Rating:**

Alternate titles: *Shojo no harawata; Guts of a Virgin; Entrails of a Whore*

激烈─血しぶきエクスタシー!!

処女のはらわた

もう、これ以上の恐怖はない。もう、これ以上の快感はない。

鮮血に彩られた暴力と官能の一夜
いま、あなたはおぞましいほどのエロスを体験する!

Like the late, great, Joe D'Amato, Japanese filmmaker Kazuo Komizu will most likely be remembered as an audacious exploitation filmmaker who wasn't afraid to merge porn and horror. D'Amato's magnum opus in this particular area was **Porno Holocaust**, Komizu's the infamous "Guts" trilogy (**Entrails of a Virgin**, **Entrails of a Beautiful Woman**, and the seemingly out of place **Female Inquisitor**)—and while neither group of films will ever be seen by the mainstream, both men have certainly assured their place in the annals of cult cinema history.

Komizu's films fall into a distinctly Japanese canon known as the "Ero-Gro" films—which stands for "erotic-grotesque". Films in this subgenre tend to operate under the notion that if gore is good, and sex is better, then combining them is invariably the greatest idea since the conception of the Reese's Peanut Butter Cup. The only problem with this is trying to find that ever-elusive balance between gore and pornography—something Komizu never quite manages to hit in this outing.

The film opens up interestingly enough with three men taking pictures of several female models. It's one of those softcore-type shoots, with the women all glistening wet, exposing their breasts, and posing in lurid "come hither" positions. To keep the audience from getting bored, the action keeps cutting to a fairly graphic sex scene, wherein one of the photographers has sex with one of the models—while photographing her during the intercourse. Afterwards, he dumps her, and she's distraught—which is a plot twist that will sort of come into play later.

After packing up for the day, our intrepid heroes set out for home. Unfortunately, it's very foggy out, and after nearly having an accident, they stop and find a deserted cabin in the forest. From here, things get really bizarre. After several drinks, two of the men encourage the third to entertain them with some wrestling. He strips down, rips the clothes off of one of the unwilling women, and begins to put her into a series of painful looking moves—while she begs him to stop. Eventually, she wets herself and passes out. The wrestler guy is upset with his buddies for making him wrestle the woman, and he heads outside—where he runs into the giant man/swamp beast who beats him about the head with a hammer causing his eyeballs to shoot out.

At this point, the film follows the standard Joe Bob Briggs' "spam in a cabin" formula—although in a far more graphic sexual manner than any U.S. film of the same subgenre. The men force themselves on the women, despite their protestations, degrading them in just about every way possible...then they all meet the swamp monster, who has a gigantic penis and shows them all new meanings to the term "degradation" as he rapes and murders the women, and just plain kills the men.

Director Kazuo Komizu (who works under the pseudonym Gaira, which astute monster film fans will recognize as the name of the beast from **War of the Gargantuas**) has managed to make a formulaic "people in the woods stalked by a monster" movie and make it fairly entertaining instead of simply rehashing other films in the subgenre. There's nothing all that new here, but Gaira is clearly having fun with the subject matter—piling on tons of sex, sleazy exploitation, and outrageously gross set-pieces in order to repulse the viewer. Still, there are some artistic elements to the direction as well. Gaira uses several humorous insert scenes during the gore sequences—which, while not all that impressive visually, are entertaining in their audacity.

**Entrails** features an ensemble cast—many of whom never worked again. The performances are nothing to write home about—everyone here's completely unlikable, which I think was what Gaira was going for. It often appears as though the cast was chosen more for their willingness to do the extended sex scenes than because they possessed any real acting ability—not that I'm really complaining. The women came across as annoying, the men loutish pigs, and the swamp monster...well, he was okay, I suppose. Sort of reminded me of a pissed off version of DC Comics' **The Swamp Thing**.

The swamp monster gets the film's funniest line, too. When one of the women asks him why he's killing all of them, he deadpans the reply "Because I hate you." Funny to think of a guy who lives in a swamp and spends his free time running around raping and murdering people making those kind of social judgments, but I think he was right on the money...I didn't like these people either.

With a title like ***Entrails of a Virgin***, you'd expect this film to deliver gore by the bucketload—and you'd be somewhat disappointed. The film gives us far more sex than gore...sex that's harder than the average Cinemax softcore, but stops short of being out and out porn. The Japanese couldn't show any genital shots in their films, therefore, in any scene where there's sex, they blur out the crotch areas. To say that it's disconcerting would be a major understatement...it's downright annoying. Of course, if a guy wants to cup his hand over the female's groin that's okay to show. Doesn't make much sense, does it?

But I digress. There is some gore here, but unfortunately, a lot of it looks pretty cheap. The guy who takes the hammer to the head looks okay...until his eyes pop out. A guy gets impaled on a javelin, a woman makes out with a severed head, before masturbating furiously with an amputated arm. A woman gets doused in swamp monster sperm, before the beast sticks his arm up through her vagina and pulls out her intestines (hence part of the title—it should be noted that this woman isn't a virgin, though). Still, gore fans should find more than enough here to hold their interest—between the gore and the sex, there's a lot of sleaze on display.

***Entrails of a Virgin*** is an entertaining little slasher/gore/exploitation film from Japan—a country that *knows* all about exploitation films. It's not a five star masterpiece, but it is entertaining--especially if you like a lot of sex and naked women to go along with your onscreen carnage. Oh yeah, and before I forget to mention it, make sure you watch the entire credits, as there's one of those infamous "after the credits" shots here. Anyway, if you're a fan of weird gore/sleaze/exploitation, Japanese horror, or splattery erotica, then ***Entrails of a Virgin*** is well worth tracking down.

# Chapter Twenty-Four

# EVIL DEAD 2: DEAD BY DAWN

**Directed by: Sam Raimi**

**Barf Bag Rating:**

EVIL DEAD 2
DEAD BY DAWN
RENAISSANCE PICTURES Presents
EVIL DEAD 2
Starring BRUCE CAMPBELL  With SARAH BERRY  DAN HICKS  KASSIE WESLEY  RICHARD DOMEIER
Music By JOSEPH LO DUCA  Special Makeup Effects MARK SHOSTROM  Edited By KAYE DAVIS
Director of Photography PETER DEMING  Executive Producers IRVIN SHAPIRO  ALEX De BENEDETTI
Written By SAM RAIMI  SCOTT SPIEGEL  Produced By ROBERT TAPERT  Directed By SAM RAIMI

Bruce Campbell is back as lovable demon killer Ash in this, the second installment of the **_Evil Dead_** series.

Released in 1987, **_Evil Dead 2_** is more of a remake than an actual sequel. While the first film had Ash and a group of friends traveling to a remote country cabin and unleashing a horde of Kandarian demons, this time around it's just him and his girlfriend, Linda. After arriving at the cabin, Ash stumbles across a tape player—one containing the translations of passages from the Necronomicon Ex Mortis, aka The Book of the Dead—a book bound in human flesh and inked in human blood. As the cabin's previous inhabitant recites the passages, the evil dead awake...forcing Ash to do battle with the forest's evil inhabitants.

Unlike the first film, which had a decidedly horror feel, **_Evil Dead 2_** goes for a more slapstick approach. One-liners and corny puns fly as fast and furious as the copious amounts of gore Raimi and company continually bathe the actors in. And while the tone is certainly lighter than in the first film, there are still a few good jump scares intermingled in the film's narrative as well.

Raimi pulls out every trick in the book and the end result is a wild, roller coaster ride of a film. Everything from miniatures, to puppets, to claymation, to stop motion animation, to rear projection is used here, and while much of it looks decidedly cheesy, it certainly adds to the film's overall effect. Raimi also relies heavily on weird camera movements and first person perspective for the evil dead themselves. The director grabs a camera and runs like a madman in one of the film's early sequences, chasing Campbell through the cabin, bursting through doors, running behind the walls and eventually ending up outside before retreating back into the forest—all of this done in one continuous take. It's nothing less than the hyper-stylized kind of direction that cult fans have come to expect from Raimi—something that's sorely missing from his recent mainstream films.

Yet, even with all of Raimi's visual flourishes, **_Evil Dead 2_** would fall flat without the performance of Bruce Campbell. Campbell is the film's true center—a character who's so ordinary that every guy in the audience identifies with him, yet so cool that we all long to be him. Whether it's firing off one-liners or slicing up demons, Campbell is amazing. And while a lot of folks look at him as little more than one of the genre's most competent and intriguing B movie actors, he's actually a solid thespian capable of pulling off serious roles as well (witnessed through his guest starring performance on **Homicide: Life on the Streets**).

Campbell carries much of the film, spending almost the entire first half trapped in the cabin on his own. Even though there's no one for him to work with, this is the best part of Campbell's performance as he demonstrates a great propensity for pulling off some Three Stooges-style physical comedy. He fights with his own hand (after it's possessed through a bite from a dismembered head), gouging his own eyes, flipping himself onto the floor, and even smashing plates over his head. It's a fantastic performance—entertaining throughout the course of the movie.

The guys at KNB did most of the FX make-up, and it's just what you'd expect for this kind of film—cheesy and gruesome. There are lots of stabbings, demons, geysers of blood, and tree monsters here...and while gross, it's usually humorous as well. For example, in one gruesome sequence, a demon's head is wedged between the floor and a board. As Ash jumps on it, trying to force it back into the basement, one of its eyeballs pops out—shooting across the room and into the screaming mouth of a woman. On the other hand, this psuedo-remake doesn't feature the infamous "tree rape" scene from the first film. While it's not as gory as Peter Jackson's **Dead Alive**, there is enough carnage to satisfy even the most discerning gore fans.

**Evil Dead 2** is a classic cult horror film in every sense of the word. Even though I find it inferior to the original (I like it, but it's a little too light-hearted for my tastes) it's certainly the film that put Sam Raimi on the map with most mainstream filmgoers. It's basically just a rehashing of the first film, with little in the way of plot, yet it works because Campbell is so perfect in his role and Raimi's style of filmmaking is so much fun to watch. The movie rips along at a furious pace, finally reaching a climax that, like the rest of the film, is so absurd that it's actually entertaining—and it sets up the sequel, **Army of Darkness**, perfectly. If you're any fan of cult cinema or a serious horror buff, then you've undoubtedly already seen this film. If you're new to the genre, or just looking for something wild and different to watch at your next get together, grab ***Evil Dead 2: Dead by Dawn***. In a word, it's "groovy."

# CHAPTER TWENTY-FIVE

# EVIL DEAD TRAP (1988)

**Directed by: Toshiharu Ikeda**

**Barf Bag Rating:**

Alternate titles: *Shiryo no wana; Evil Dead's Trap (1998) (Canada: festival title English title)*

A TOSHIHARU IKEDA FILM
EVIL DEAD TRAP
UNEARTHED CLASSICS

When late night talk show host Nami (Miyuki Ono) gets a videotape submission for her show, she pops it into the VCR to see what one of her fans has sent her. What she discovers is far more than she'd bargained for—the tape contains footage of an Asian woman being brutally murdered in an abandoned building. The coup de grace is when our unseen assailant stabs the young woman in the eye with a sharp knife (in a scene that would have made Lucio Fulci and Salvador Dali squeal with delight)—shot in loving close-up and featuring lots of eyeball fluid.

If that weren't enough, the assailant is even kind enough to videotape driving directions to his location—apparently in the hopes that Nami will come pay him a visit. Not one to disappoint (or pass up a potentially good news story), Nami loads up three of her girlfriends and an assistant director and heads off to find the location featured on the tape. It is a decision that will have life-altering repercussions.

Toshiharu Ikeda's **Evil Dead Trap** has long been considered one of the best Japanese slasher films, and for good reason—it's unrelentingly brutal, gory, has a veritable truckload of atmosphere, is stylishly directed, and features enough crass exploitation elements to keep even the hardcore fans happy. In fact, it would be one of the greatest slasher films ever if not for an entirely out of left field ending that drags on for too long and doesn't fit with the tone of the rest of the film. Ah, but at least it's really good up until that point...

Ikeda's film owes a great deal to the cinema of Dario Argento, with little flourishes from the works of men like Lucio Fulci and David Cronenberg thrown in for good measure. Some viewers and critics cite this as a bad thing—a decision that confounds me to no end. It makes very little sense to bash **Evil Dead Trap** for being unoriginal—particularly when the entire slasher subgenre is filled with films that simply riff on the films that have come before them.

Even more confusing is the disdain for the Argento-esque nature of the film. Personally, I'm of the opinion that if you're going to "borrow" from another filmmaker, you should make sure you appropriate elements from someone who's really good—and who's better at these kinds of films than Dario Argento?

Simply put, ***Evil Dead Trap*** is the closest anyone's ever come to mimicking the pitch and tone of Argento's own cinema. It's not a perfect re-creation of the auteur's work (Ikeda injects enough of his own aesthetic sensibilities into the mix to keep the film from becoming a pure homage), but in a horror universe filled with really bad movies, why fans would rebel against someone trying to make films like one of the masters of the form is beyond me. It's confusing at best, and misguided at worst.

Ikeda's film features a variety of strengths—from the excellent gore work, to the ever-increasing level of tension, to a score that sounds as if Claudio Simonetti and Goblin composed it themselves. Things race along quite brilliantly until the hour-and-five-minute mark, where the third act begins and the whole film devolves into a weird experience that doesn't have much in common with what's come before it.

During this phase, things become surreal and supernatural as one character gives birth to their own split personality. This sets up a drawn out final showdown that seems to feature more discussion than action. And, invariably, this sets up the infamous final twist scene, wherein the film runs with its Cronenbergian influence.

It should be noted that ***Evil Dead Trap*** has spawned two sequels to date—neither of which has anything to do with the original.

Still, don't let the whacked out ending put you off—***Evil Dead Trap*** is an unrepentantly violent piece of slasher cinema that more than delivers the goods for the first two acts. The gore, once it actually makes its way into the story, comes fast, furious, and in inventive ways.

Aside from the snuff footage, one woman is impaled on a series of sharp spikes, another is bound to a Rube Goldberg-esque booby trap that eventually sees her getting smashed in the side of the head with a machete, another woman is garroted, and a guy takes a spike through the head. The gore work is sure to please—which is part of the reason why I love this film so much.

I'm still not really sure how anyone who considers themselves a hardcore horror fan could hate this film—but I know the detractors are out there. However, don't let them put you off tracking down a copy of this classic film. While **Evil Dead Trap** is not a perfect horror movie, it does so many things well that anyone even remotely interested in slasher cinema should make it a priority to see it.

# CHAPTER TWENTY-SIX

# THE GATES OF HELL (1980)

**Directed by: Lucio Fulci**

**Barf Bag Rating:**

Alternate titles: *City of the Living Dead (1980); Paura nella città dei morti viventi; Fear in the City of the Living Dead (1980); Fear, The (1980/II) Pater Thomas (1980)(Europe: bootleg title); Twilight of the Dead (1980)*

"THE DEAD SHALL RISE AND WALK THE EARTH"
CHARLES HAMM
1809 - 1847
A FILM BY
LUCIO FULCI
THE GATES OF
HELL

One thing that becomes readily apparent when viewing ***The Gates Of Hell*** is that legendary Italian director Lucio Fulci is no Argento, Mario Bava, or Michele Soavi. Sure, Fulci's a competent filmmaker who has a fairly distinguished filmography (including ***The Beyond***, ***House By The Cemetery***, and ***New York Ripper***), but ultimately he lacks the stylistic flourishes that are so inherent in both Argento and Soavi's best work--one of the key elements that makes Euro-horror so much fun to watch.

Looking a lot like a rough draft for Fulci's later film, ***The Beyond***, ***The Gates Of Hell*** tells the story of Dunwich Massachusetts, a small town where a priest commits suicide in the local cemetery. This event opens the gates of hell, allowing the dead to return and walk the earth. . .unless a reporter, a psychic, and a psychologist can close them before the impending All Saint's Day holiday. In the meantime, lots of weird things start happening, all usually accompanied by an appearance of the dead priest, who's generally hanging from his noose like some kind of satanic piñata.

The performances are actually pretty decent, considering the insipid dialogue that was written into the script. Genre veteran Christopher George turns in the best performance as Peter Bell, the aforementioned reporter. Fulci regular Catriona MacColl plays Mary, the psychic, and Carlo de Mejo tackles the role of Jerry, the psychiatrist. Italian horror icon John Morghen (AKA Giovanni Lombardo Radice) once again demonstrates that he's the hardest dying man in showbiz, this time playing the sexual deviant Bob--who takes an industrial-sized drill bit through the head. Also featured in a small role is none other than auteur Michele Soavi, playing a back alley Romeo who meets with our demonic priest in one the film's most famous scenes.

Gino de Rossi handles the special effects duties, with varying degrees of success. ***The Gates Of Hell*** is widely remembered for two gore sequences: the John Morghen drill bit to the head and the even more infamous girl ralphing her intestines scene. Both of these are great sequences and well worthy of their infamy. Some of the other FX, however, are more laughable than anything. When the zombies rip off several characters' scalps in order to get at their brains, the effect is undeniably lame. Equally unimpressive is the zombie make-up itself--it appears as if de Rossi decided to do nothing other than glue oatmeal to the actors' faces to make them look lumpy and undead. Needless to say, it has less than the desired effect, as I found myself giggling any time one of these undead monsters appeared on the screen.

Speaking of monsters "appearing" on the screen, the film has the hysterically bad habit of having the zombies possess what appears to be the ability to teleport. One second they're there--then poof, they're gone, only to re-appear a few seconds later...somewhere else. I don't mind a guy taking liberty with the established rules, but I would like to know what the rules are beforehand. Zombies simply don't teleport where I come from.

Also delightfully entertaining is the foley work. Foleys, for those of you not familiar with the term, are the guys who watch the film and add the sound effects. There are lots of worms and maggots in this movie, none of which make any noticeable sound in the real world. But, here in Fulci-land, they screech and squeak and squish along, all pretty noisily, in fact. What's even worse though are the sound effects when our heroes prepare to enter the underground cemetery. Here, we're treated to various wilderness sounds, including the screeching of monkeys--in New England, no less.

Fabio Frizzi's score is appropriately "Goblin-esque", managing to be both synth-heavy and gothic at same time. What seems to work against it the most isn't anything to do with Frizzi's ability as a composer, but more because of Vincenzo Tomassi and Lucio Fulci's sloppy editing. Like most of Fulci's films, **The Gates Of Hell** features an abundance of rough edits, jumping from one scene to another with little warning and no real transition. In this film, we can be watching a scene with a zombie, Frizzi's score pounding along, then suddenly jump to another unrelated scene--which has no music at all. What makes the effect even more jarring is that Frizzi's score isn't gradually faded out before the jump, nor is it even at a point where you can cut away from it effectively. No, Fulci just jumps to the next scene, cutting off the music in mid-note.

The direction is what we've come to expect from Fulci--meaning there's lot of zoom-in shots of actors' eyes, leering zoom shots of any gore effect, and a generally workmanlike approach to the genre that's really out of line with his compatriots such as Argento. Notably missing from the film is the Fulci gore staple, brutal eye violence. Fulci is the king of ocular mayhem, generally featuring at least one eyeball removal/impalement/etc. in each of his films. No such luck here.

What is perhaps most aggravating about this film (aside from the ending, which I'll get to shortly) is that half the scenes are so poorly lit that you can't see what's happening. Everything else that I've commented on up to this point still manages to make the movie campy fun, but this is my one legitimate beef with this movie. When the characters go down into the cemetery near the end, they're surrounded by the newly risen dead...of course, you can't really see any of the dead, but you know they're there because they eventually pop into frame. Watching this flick is like watching TV with a black sheet over the screen. It's frustrating, to say the least.

The film features one of those infamous "twist" endings, and it's one that pretty much sucks. I won't spoil it for you here, but I will defend Fulci. Apparently, Fulci shot a better ending, but someone spilled coffee/embalming fluid/whatever on the footage. Fulci didn't have time to reshoot, so he did the best he could with what was left.

Fulci and frequent collaborator Dardano Sacchetti co-wrote the film's script and it's a real howler. The dialogue is unbelievably bad, with characters basically covering all the exposition through idle chatter. Early on, Mary witnesses the Father's suicide during a seance. She screams and apparently dies of fright. Later, reporter Bell hears her screaming from inside her coffin and frees her with a pickaxe (good thing the funeral homes in New York don't use embalming fluid, eh?).

The town of Dunwich doesn't appear on any map, yet at one point, the locals are listening to the radio where the announcer mentions that not only is Dunwich a town, but it's also the name of the county. To complicate matters further, Dunwich is supposedly built on the ruins of Salem Massachusetts--interesting since Salem is still there. These are just a few of the unintentionally hilarious moments in the film...rest assured, there are many more left for you to discover on your own.

I know it must seem like I dislike this movie, but I don't. In fact, I love ***The Gates Of Hell*** quite a bit. It's not a good horror film by traditional metrics, but it's one of those great pieces of schlock that's endearing nevertheless. If you've never seen a Fulci flick before, I'd recommend starting with ***The Beyond*** or ***Zombi***, two of his more impressive offerings. If you do see ***The Gates Of Hell*** first, I can only hope that you won't allow it to color your perceptions of the man's work too badly. Despite his misfirings, Fulci was certainly capable of making some good horror films.

# CHAPTER TWENTY-SEVEN

# GUINEA PIG: DEVIL'S EXPERIMENT (1985)

**Directed by: Hideshi Hino**

**Barf Bag Rating:**

Alternate titles: *Za ginipiggu: Akuma no jikken; Guinea Pig*

GUINEA PIG
DEVILS EXPERIMENT
ANDROID OF NOTRE DAME
UNEARTHED FILMS DOUBLE FEATURE DVD

In 1985, Japanese manga artist Hideshi Hino started his infamous ***Guinea Pig*** series of short gore vignettes with the release of ***Devil's Experiment***. Relegated to obscurity for years because of its subject matter and because the short essentially has zero redeeming qualities, the film was something that only the hardest of hardcore gorehounds experienced firsthand—until the early 2000s when Stephen Biro's Unearthed Films brought these legendary titles to American audiences.

Simply put, this first entry in the series is easily one of the more wild films covered in this book. It's not as gory as some of the titles herein, but it definitely has a mean-spirited vibe that's bound to linger with you for days after watching it.

What makes ***Devil's Experiment*** so disturbing can be attributed to a number of factors.

First, the subject matter itself is bothersome. Three Japanese men capture a young woman and torture her until she dies. End of story. There's no real plot at work in ***Devil's Experiment***—the film exists solely as an exercise in extreme exploitation. No one has a name, no actors are listed, there are no credits. It's just 40 minutes of torture and gore.

This is, no doubt, part of what led to the misguided belief that ***Devil's Experiment*** was actually a real snuff film. To the uninitiated, it's possible that the film could be viewed as real, I suppose. However, anyone with any kind of background in watching gore cinema, knowledge of special effects, or just plain observant viewers will spot that the film is clearly fiction. Disturbing fiction, yes, but still make believe.

Second, the film's effects work is impressive for the most part. The young woman in the film is kicked, slapped, forced to listen to white noise for 20 hours, has scalding water poured on her, has maggots placed on the festering wound, is pinched with pliers, has her fingernail ripped out, takes a sledgehammer to the hand, and has her eyeball penetrated by a needle. With the exception of the hand, the slapping, and the kicking, all of these things look pretty real. While our main actress often seems more subdued than you'd expect in any given situation (meaning if someone poured scalding hot water on me, I'd scream for hours on end), it almost works in the film's favor.

And the reason it works in the film's favor is reason number three for why **Devil's Experiment** is such a harrowing viewing experiment: the film is nihilistically bleak and hopeless.

The lack of a plot, identifiable characters, or any of the other narrative conventions of traditional cinema continually add to the documentary or snuff film feel of the vignette. The sets are sparse, the acting is minimal, and there's barely a soundtrack or any sort of camera technique to the action. Because of this, viewers can easily start to assume that what they're seeing is in fact real, and that there can't possibly be a happy "Hollywood ending" in store for this young woman.

Ultimately, though, what makes **Guinea Pig: Devil's Experiment** such a classic piece of exploitation cinema is the way it lingers with you for years after it's ended. While it may not be real, there's no doubt that if snuff cinema existed, it would probably look something like this. With this film, Hideshi Hino has glimpsed into the heart of darkness, shown his audience a portrait of what he saw, but offered nothing in the way of redemption or catharsis. This may fly in the face of conventional cinema, but it draws a chilling picture of the way things generally work in the real world. It's easy to dismiss **Devil's Experiment** as a piece of trash cinema designed solely to appeal to those with a geek show mentality—but that doesn't mean it's still not worth seeing for folks looking for something beyond what passes for horror in mainstream cinema.

# CHAPTER TWENTY-EIGHT

# GUINEA PIG: FLOWER OF FLESH AND BLOOD (1985)

**Directed by: Hideshi Hino**

**Barf Bag Rating:**

Alternate titles: *Za ginipiggu 3: Chiniku no hana; Flowers of Flesh and Blood (1985) (V); Guinea Pig: Flowers of Flesh and Blood (1985) (V)*

GUINEA PIG
FLOWER OF
FLESH AND BLOOD
MAKING OF GUINEA PIG
UNEARTHED FILMS
DOUBLE FEATURE
DVD

***Cannibal Holocaust***. ***Salo: The 120 Days of Sodom***. ***Cannibal Ferox***. All are films that have an infamous reputation amongst fans of disturbing underground cinema—films that mainstream moviegoers would never watch, if for no other reason than because they're too violent, too disturbing, or even too gross. Yet, there are followings for each of these films—cults of fans who revere these movies and the men who made them. The films live on, available in the cult sections of independent video stores, talked about in fanzines, and lusted after by viewers with a taste for something a little more extreme.

Yet, for all the hoopla surrounding these films, they all tend to pale in comparison when talking about the ***Guinea Pig*** series from Japan. Why is that? Well, for starters it's because no matter how extreme the films I mentioned earlier are, it's always clear that they're films. If things get too hairy for you, you can always remind yourself that "it's only a movie." And while some installments in the ***Guinea Pig*** series of films certainly play as short films, others, like ***Flower of Flesh and Blood*** do not.

It is this blurring of the line between reality and cinema that has earned the film such a cult following—both here in America and abroad—and what inspired actor Charlie Sheen to turn his copy over to the FBI in the early 1990s, believing it was a legitimate snuff film. The subsequent investigation, by both the FBI and Japanese authorities (which included stopping by to have a chat with *Deep Red* magazine editor Chas. Balun) revealed what anyone with half a clue about gore films and moviemaking already knew—that ***Flower of Flesh and Blood*** was a gruesome exercise in gore and Japanese exploitation, but that it was also fiction.

***Flower of Flesh and Blood*** certainly plays like what a legitimate snuff film might look like—it's got essentially one set (a closed room), one victim, and one sadistic Japanese man dressed up in period samurai garb. There's little here in the way of plot, which only adds to the confusion for extremely naïve splatter film fans.

The nearly forty-five minute long short opens on a street in Japan. A camera follows the progress of a pretty young Asian girl as she goes about her day. The film cuts several more times, showing her in different locations, largely oblivious to the fact that she's being stalked. Finally, as night falls, she realizes that she's being followed. She attempts to flee, but doesn't manage to escape.

When we next see the girl, she's unconscious, tied down to a bed in small and dingy little room. We see her assailant for the first time, a Japanese man with horrible looking teeth and dressed in samurai gear. He's sharpening a knife, which he then uses to kill a chicken over the girl. From here, things get pretty intense.

Our samurai drugs his victim, putting her into a state where she's still barely conscious, but doesn't feel any pain. The victim, who's about to bloom into the flower of flesh and blood, must be aware of the process of transformation, and welcome it in a kind drug induced euphoria, apparently.

With his victim now prepared, the samurai strips her naked, then begins dismembering her piece by piece on the bed. We're treated to a hand amputation, the removal of the arm at the shoulder (complete with chisel and hammer to break through the bone, adding a nicely realistic touch to the proceedings), and removal of both legs (where you can hear the saw cutting its way through bone—another nice touch).

Finally, we see the samurai open the chest cavity and remove the intestines and internal organs—a scene intercut with close-ups of the girl's face as she vomits blood and finally dies. However, our samurai isn't done yet—he continues on with his ritual, chopping off the head, the removing one of the eyes, which he then licks and devours.

The transformation complete, the samurai has a cigarette while the camera shows us trophies from previous encounters. Then the film freeze frames on the shot of another girl on the streets of Japan and fades to black—letting us know that samurai is still out there.

The film was helmed by Japanese manga (comic book) artist Hideshi Hino. Hino's film is a stark and unrelenting viewing experience for sure, but hardly something that should be mistaken for the genuine article when it comes to snuff cinema.

There are countless things that should indicate to anyone with a background in filmmaking or film viewing that this is a fictional production and not some homemade video of real murder. ***Flower of Flesh and Blood*** contains not only a soundtrack (admittedly minimalistic, but a soundtrack nonetheless), but also some fancy edits (including multiple angles of some scenes), slow-motion, point-of-view shots (including one from the chicken's perspective), and also credits. All are techniques that would be missing from a legitimate snuff film—provided that such a thing even existed to begin with.

To Hino's credit, he does do a good job of blurring the line between fantasy and reality for much of the running time. While ***Flower of Flesh and Blood*** is clearly a twisted piece of cinematic fiction, it still can hit you right in the balls with its unrelenting depravity. I've always said that the Japanese make some of the most twisted exploitation cinema in the world, and this tape only confirms that notion. ***Flower*** is a disturbing piece of cinema that is definitely not for mainstream consumption and might even disturb some of the more jaded fans of hardcore gore out there.

Invariably, the thing that gets the most praise from fans of this film is the effects work, which is quite impressive for the most part. To an undiscerning horror fan, the effects here are really good—and the added touches, like the sound of the saw grinding on bone and the hammer and chisel working the shoulder free only add to the effect. However, those more familiar with the workings of gore FX will undoubtedly spot some scenes and sequences that are clearly staged. A shot of a knife opening the stomach cavity looks particularly fake, with it being clear that all of the blood is coming from the dummy knife and not the wound itself. The blood and viscera itself looks a little suspect as well, but not so bad that it detracts from the atmosphere overall. At any rate, I mention these things solely to show that while the FX work is good, it's not without a few flaws.

Overall, ***Guinea Pig: Flower of Flesh and Blood*** deserves the reputation it's received. This is an intense and disturbing little vignette with numerous artistic touches designed to make it play as more than a simple gore piece. Few will see it for anything other than the gore, but it's nice that there's at least an attempt at adding some kind of dimension. The special effects are impressive, the film technique solid, and the overall end result is a short film that will leave you bothered by its imagery for a long time after the screen fades to black. You can't ask for much more than that.

# CHAPTER TWENTY-NINE

# GUINEA PIG: MERMAID IN A MANHOLE (1988)

**Directed by: Hideshi Hino**

**Barf Bag Rating:**

Alternate title: *Za ginipiggu 4: Manhoru no naka no ningyo*

GUINEA PIG
MERMAID IN A MANHOLE
HE NEVER DIES
UNEARTHED FILMS
DOUBLE FEATURE
DVD

This fourth installment in the famed *Guinea Pig* series is something of a departure from the previous entries. While the first two films caused uproar when it was believed they were actual snuff films, *Mermaid in a Manhole* never had such a problem. Why, you ask? Because this episode features a real plot that clearly marks the onscreen action as fiction.

*Mermaid in a Manhole* is only slightly less gory than previous films in the series, but it is far more profound than either *Flower of Flesh and Blood* or *Devil's Experiment*. Director Hideshi Hino once again seems to take a ghoulish delight in decay, dismemberment, and the more ghastly elements of life (and death), but rather than focus on evil (the carnage in both of the earlier films is perpetrated by human monsters), he instead concentrates on love, devotion, and longing...all with a healthy dose of the gross stuff mixed in for good measure.

Shigeru Saiki is a painter living alone in Japan. His wife has recently left him, and he's struggling to find artistic inspiration. Hoping to find his muse, the artist spends each day wandering in the sewers near his flat. This sewer was once a beautiful river, where Saiki played as a child. Even more impressive, he swears that he once saw a mermaid frolicking in the water.

One of his trips into the this netherworld proves his childhood belief was right—the mermaid lives. However, the years of living in sewage instead of clean water has taken a toll on her. Our artist takes her back to his apartment, stores her in his bathtub, and tries to not only resume painting, but nurse her back to health.

Unfortunately, the effects of the sewer are too much for the mermaid to overcome. Her health deteriorates, and gruesome lesions form all over her body. Knowing she's about to die, she asks the artist to capture her condition in his painting. The artist agrees, and begins work on her portrait. As her condition worsens, the bond between the two grows stronger. Unable to find just the right color, the mermaid tells the painter to use the pus from her wounds—which he does in order to finish the painting.

In all honesty, *Mermaid in a Manhole* works best when viewed as a twisted fairy tale. Rather than existing solely to gross out an audience, or a cautionary fable about monsters living amongst us, ***Mermaid*** seems far more interested in the lofty aspirations of making a statement about the nature of relationships and devotion—with a healthy dose of Cronenberg's fascination with human decay tossed in to keep things interesting.

Because of this, ***Mermaid in a Manhole*** transcends being simple splatter cinema—it's gross, but it's also touching and a little bittersweet as well. Don't let this put you off seeing it, though—the gore is good. Everything else is just bonus.

Unfortunately, while the ***Guinea Pig*** series would spawn more sequels, this was the last of the truly great ones. Some of the later installments aren't so much gory as weird, which certainly lessened the impact of the series for the hardcore fans who'd been around since day one. Despite this, all three volumes covered in this guide are classic entries—and well worth having in a permanent collection of gore cinema.

# CHAPTER THIRTY

# GUTS OF A BEAUTY (1986)

**Director: Kazuo "Gaira" Komizu**

**Barf Bag Ring:**

Alternate titles: *Bijo no harawata; Entrails of a Beautiful Woman; Guts of a Virgin 2*

肉をちぎれ！
骨までしゃぶれ！
激烈——血しぶき
恐怖と戦慄の超ド級官能ホラー。スプラッタ＆エロス第2弾!!
美女のはらわた
うえ沢めぐみ●石井絢子／北川香織●主演●主演 健／関川慎二／佐野和宏／草加 力／吉江芳成 ほか
監督・脚本・カイラ●製作・八月春波●配給 にっかつ 成人映画

Proving once again that no one outdoes the Japanese when it comes to pure sleaze is 1986's ***Guts of a Beauty***—another "ero-gro" (the slang term for Japan's "Erotic Grotesque" subgenre) film filled to the brim with rape, gore, drug use, rape, murder, a hermaphrodite zombie, rape, wild sex, and even a few rapes thrown in for good measure. You have to give the Japanese credit—when they make an exploitation flick, they don't pussyfoot around the exploitation elements.

This cinematic masterpiece was helmed by none other than Kazuo "Gaira" Komizu, the legendary splatter auteur behind ***Entrails of a Virgin*** and ***Living Dead in Tokyo Bay***. Unfortunately, this film isn't nearly as good as ***Entrails***, but it does feature just enough gruesome carnage and sleaze to get included in this guide.

The plot in ***Guts of a Beauty*** makes ***Entrails of a Virgin*** look like high art in comparison.

A young woman goes looking for her missing sister. This search leads her to her sister's yakuza "boyfriend"—except that said boyfriend has sold the missing sister into sex slavery. Never one to let a good business opportunity pass, the yakuza heavy figures if the first sister was good enough to export, so is this one. Before you know it, our virginal young woman is being raped by the yakuza henchmen. To really get her in the mood, they give her a shot of Angel Rain—a special, high quality drug guaranteed to get her engine running. Unfortunately for the yakuza, the woman escapes and confesses everything to nearby psychiatrist (Seira Kitagawa) before jumping to her death.

Shifting gears, Gaira now decides to follow the psychiatrist as she plots revenge against the gangsters. Her nefarious plan involves hypnotizing one of the henchmen and programming him to kill his cohorts. Good idea, only it backfires...and soon our new heroine is being gang raped by the same goons as the first girl. Angel Rain is too much for her, though, and she promptly dies. Of course, death is only the beginning in a Gaira film, and she merges forms with the dismembered corpse of her yakuza buddy and turns into a giant hermaphroditic zombie bent on revenge.

The rest of the film is the quest for vengeance, complete with several fun gore sequences that everyone's been waiting for. Splatter fans will finally have reason to rejoice as our zombie monster rapes and pillages its way through the yakuza ranks.

As mentioned before, *Guts of a Beauty* isn't a particularly good film, even by Gaira standards. While the idea of mixing sex and gore is an admirable one, the director never quite gets the balance right—meaning that this film features interminably long scenes of softcore coupling (the Japanese viewed the showing of pubic hair as an obscenity until 1996—hence any genital shot is optically fogged or covered by the environment) and not enough gore. In fact, most of the 70 minute running time is made up of sex scenes between the various characters in the film, while most of the gore is held off until the splatterific climax. In this regard, gore fans could easily fast forward through large chunks of this movie to get to the good stuff.

The gore effects are workmanlike and unlikely to blow anyone away with their technical mastery. However, what they lack in sophistication, they more than make up for in sheer audacity. The chest bursting penis scene (completely ripped off from Ridley Scott's *Alien*) is so cool that you can forgive almost all of the film's other flaws. Couple that with suffocation by stuffing a head up a zombie vagina, and well, you've got a winner of a movie.

If nothing else, *Guts of a Beauty* proves that you don't have to be a good movie to be a good gore film. Check your brain at the door for this one, sit back, pop a few beverages, and prepare for the sleaze. You could do far worse than this on a Friday night.

# Chapter Thirty-One

# High Tension (2003)

**Directed by: Alexandre Aja**

**Barf Bag Rating:**

Alternate titles: *Haute Tension; Switchblade Romance (2003) (International: English title)*

HIGH
TENSION

One thing becomes readily apparent to any horror fan as he watches Alexandre Aja's French horror film **Haute Tension**--this guy grew up on '80s slasher films. Aja has crafted one of the slicker looking genre films of this century, and it constantly, and consistently, pays homage to the films of his youth while still remaining its own movie.

Marie (Cecile de France) and Alex (Maiwenn Le Besco) are two college students off to visit Alex's family. Unfortunately, they're about to be terrorized by a maniac in a dilapidated truck who comes calling to the family homestead...or are they? What ensues is a tense fight for survival leading up to a twist ending that can be viewed as either outlandish or clever—and I'm still not entirely sure which way I see it.

Spoilers ahead....

The film's huge twist is that there is no psychotic truck driver—Marie herself is the killer. One's initial reaction to this revelation is to generally assume that Aja has cheated his audience—if Marie is the killer, the film has some serious plot holes that aren't ever addressed. Walking out of the theater after the screening of **Haute Tension**, this was my initial reaction.

However, I had this niggling feeling that I'd missed something. Further reflection caused me to remember the film's opening framing device—Marie in a hospital, after being put through hell. This scene may be the key to understanding **Haute Tension's** plot twist—rather than viewing the events in the film as legitimate and happening in narrative real time, one must instead look at them as memories from a clearly unreliable narrator. Much like Kevin Spacey's character in **The Usual Suspects**, Marie's story is one that simply can't be taken at face value—therefore, the plot inconsistencies almost exist as a subtle reminder that Marie is telling us the tale, and that we can't take everything she says as the truth.

That alone is interesting enough, however, Aja takes things a step farther with his well-defined love for horror movies. **Haute Tension** appears to be an elaborate homage to a number of different genre films. The truck driver looks a bit like a gone-to-seed Michael Myers (if he ditched the Shatner mask and moved to France); he acts a bit like Rusty Nail from **Joy Ride**; he drives a truck not unlike the one The Creeper cruises around in while stalking his prey in *Jeepers Creepers*; a bathroom stalking sequence is lifted almost directly from William Lustig's *Maniac*; the majority of the film has a great deal in common with Dean Koontz's *Intensity*; etc.

The question is, are all of these things simply ideas that Aja wanted to pay homage to in his film, or are they instead another sly way of telling the audience that Marie is making up all of these elements? There's no hint ever offered in the film that Marie is a fan of horror cinema, but is it really a stretch to imagine that she's included numerous horror film elements to her story in order to make it play as more believable and to portray herself in a better light? After all, she is supposedly a virgin, as the early dialogue points out—and aren't the virgins always the survivors of these films as opposed to the monsters?

This is the conundrum of *Haute Tension*--it's never readily apparent which scenario might be true. If initial reactions are any indication, then most people appear to be viewing the plot twist as a huge cheat on the part of the filmmaker. It's how I viewed it at first, and even now, after re-examining the film, I'm not entirely convinced that it wasn't. However, the above-mentioned plot elements certainly make a strong case for it being something more than just a weak twist in a standard horror film. It's unfortunate that the majority of *Haute Tension's* audience isn't going to be genre cinema literate enough to make that potential connection. Those of us who do, however, can certainly look at the film in a much different, and more intriguing, light.

Regardless of how you view the twist in the film's narrative, there's no denying *Haute Tension* is a pretty film to look at. Aja's use of the camera and the cinematography are quite appealing. It's never as overt as Argento or Bava's work with the camera or the lurid colors, but there's certainly some visual flair happening in the film.

The real star of *Haute Tension*, though, is Gianetto De Rossi's gore. Astute genre fans will remember Gianetto's work on Lucio Fulci gore epics like *The Beyond*, *Zombie*, etc.

De Rossi's work here isn't quite as over the top as it was in the Fulci films, but it's a welcome return to form for one of the genre's most beloved craftsmen. There's no CGI in this film—all the FX work is done the old-fashioned way, and that alone earns my respect. There are numerous standout gore sequences (including the best use of a power tool in a horror film since the original **Texas Chainsaw Massacre**), but the brutal beheading of Alex's father, and the gruesome slashing of her mother's throat are the cream of the crop as far as carnage goes. **Haute Tension** isn't a hardcore gore film, but it more than delivers the goods in terms of onscreen mayhem.

It remains to be seen whether **Haute Tension** is a decent genre film with a cop-out twist or if it's a sublime horror movie that manages to fool even its own audience. To get to the bottom of that issue, one would almost have to speak to director Aja personally—and even then, we may never really know the answer. However, there's no denying this film is intense, brutal, and lovingly filmed. That it also inspires debate and conversation is the proverbial icing on the cake.

# CHAPTER THIRTY-TWO

# ICHI THE KILLER (2001)

**Directed by: Takashi Miike**

**Barf Bag Rating:**

Alternate title: *Koroshiya 1Koroshiya ichi (2001) (Japan: alternative spelling)*

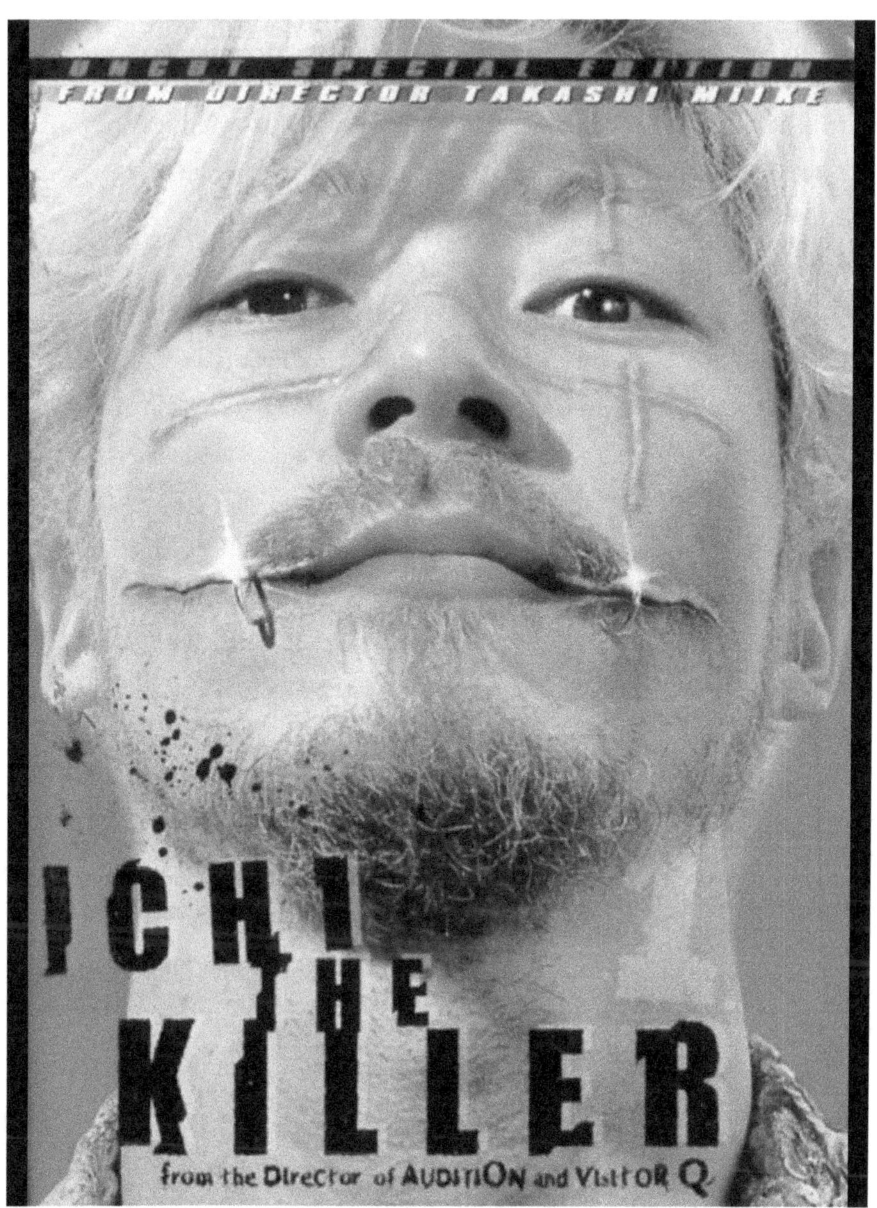
UNCUT SPECIAL EDITION
FROM DIRECTOR TAKASHI MIIKE
ICHI THE KILLER
from the Director of AUDITION and VISITOR Q

*"There is no love in your violence"*—Kakihara, ***Ichi the Killer***

Takashi Miike is basically a movie industry unto himself. The director cranks out films at a breakneck pace and has developed a rabid following here in America over the past decade or so. Most of this is attributable to two films: Audition and the one we're covering in this review: 2001's ***Ichi the Killer.***

***Ichi's*** plot is simplistic at best. A severely dysfunctional young man named Ichi (Nao Omori) becomes an assassin for hire after being hypnotized by Jijii (Shinya Tsukamoto, director of the ***Tetsuo*** films). Jijii has convinced Ichi that he was bullied as a youth, and witness to a brutal rape. This rage allows the young man to slaughter any who anger him by utilizing the twin blades hidden in the ends of his shoes.

When one of his victims is Yakuza boss Anjo, Anjo's right hand man Kakihara (played brilliantly by Tadanobu Asano) sets out to find the killer responsible. To do this, Kakihara will use his sadistic and violent tendencies to cut a swath through the entire Japanese underworld—until he finally finds Ichi for the inevitable showdown that leaves most viewers scratching their heads at the outcome.

While ***Ichi*** may be based on a manga (Japanese comic book) and looks rather cartoonish in its execution, it's a much deeper film than it appears to be. Miike may be running out of tricks technically speaking (several sequences, including a manically edited opening, are recycled from earlier films), but philosophically, he still has a lot to say.

The whacked out Yakuza underworld of Miike's Japan is populated with sadists, masochistic hookers, demented torturers, perverts, Kakihara with his wild body modifications, and regular old-school criminals who just shake their heads at the absurdity of it all (none of which is particularly original in the Miike oeuvre--***Dead or Alive*** features most of these same elements), but it's the philosophical underpinnings that really elevate ***Ichi*** above pure exploitation.

Make no mistake--***Ichi the Killer*** is a flawed film. Shot in a style that can be difficult to follow, most viewers will enjoy it on a visceral level for the gore. However, more patient cinephiles will find the deeper meanings buried under the layers of carnage. The true point of ***Ichi*** is somewhat elusive since the film throws so many themes at the viewers all at once. There's the whole love/sex/violence thing, which is arguably the most superficial of the bunch. There's some sort of statement on the futility of vengeance that comes through in spots. And one of Miike's pet themes, people who are abandoned and must make their own way in the world, turns up as well (both in Ichi himself and in the child of the Yakuza gunman who winds up dead during the climax).

So, thematically speaking, ***Ichi*** brings a lot to the table. It's a bit muddled at times, but fortunately, the gore generally kicks in and you can forget about the messages. And what gore it is...

Even in it's truncated form, this is one violent and twisted film that will please fans of movies like ***Riki-O***. Ichi chops people into pieces with savage delight, Kakihara tortures people in the most gruesome ways imaginable (including himself), and so on. The film is brutally misogynistic in spots, but Miike spreads the atrocity around...including punishing the men. In fact, the women occasionally get off easier than the men. Miike is an equal opportunity punisher, it seems.

To catalogue all the great gore in this film would be a review in itself, but the high points include Ichi slicing a man in half right down the middle, Kakihara cutting off the tip of his tongue, a sliced off nipple, and more blood and body parts than you can shake a stick at. Gore fans will love this film—it's arguably one of the most gory films I've seen in years, with some really good special effects work.

Finally, I'd be remiss if I didn't mention the cast. I'm not sure what to make of the acting in this film—it regularly vacillates between decent and horrible. However, given that the majority of the actors (including Takeshi Kitano film regular Susumu Terrajima, who makes a brief appearance) in the film have done quality work in the past, I can't help but wonder if the odd performances were by design. Given Miike's penchant for doing strange things, it wouldn't surprise me...

Ultimately, ***Ichi the Killer*** is another postcard from the abyss courtesy of Takashi Miike. The man continues to churn out gut-wrenching (but not in the traditional sense, of course) films, and this one is no exception. While it's easy to get caught up in the savage (and often amusing) violence, there's clearly more at work here than just gore for gore's sake. Miike continues to push the envelope in terms of taste and cinematic violence, and I can only imagine where he might go from here...

# CHAPTER THIRTY-THREE

# LEIF JONKER'S DARKNESS (1993)

**Director: Leif Jonker**

**Barf Bag Rating:**

Alternate title: *Darkness*

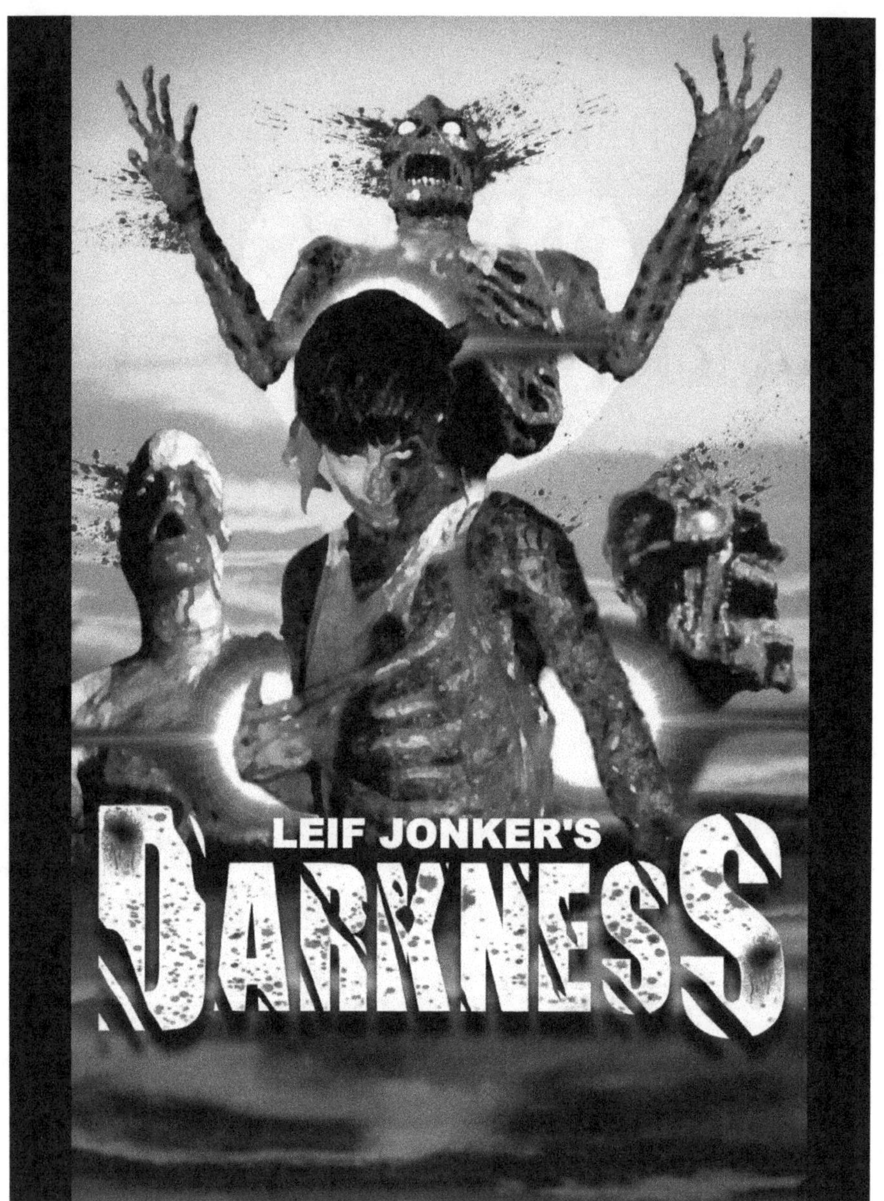
LEIF JONKER'S
DARKNESS

I'm not sure why it is, but most of the low-budget splatter films of recent years seem really fixated on zombies and serial killers. Don't get me wrong, I love the flesh-eating undead and your standard blood-craving psychopath as much as anybody—but I can't help but wish the guys making these films would branch out a bit every once in awhile.

This is at least part of the reason I liked ***Leif Jonker's Darkness*** as much as I did. Jonker skips past the *morti viventi* and psycho slashers and goes in a different direction: vampires. It seems odd that there haven't been a ton of really gory vampire films, but there haven't—which makes this one almost unique in annals of gore cinema. Of course, just having vampires in the movie doesn't make it great—the fact that it's a gory splatterfest filmed on Super 8MM (as opposed to the now standard video) that showcases the talents of a burgeoning young gore auteur is really what makes it stand out.

After bearing witness to a vampiric slaughter in a convenience store, Tobe (Gary Miller) sets out to stop the impending vampire apocalypse. His target is head bloodsucker Liven (Randall Aviks), who apparently killed Tobe's family prior to the film's opening. Unable to take on the vampires alone, Tobe enlists the aid of a group of teenagers returning from a rock concert—what ensues is a gory battle royale between man and vampire.

What is most impressive about Jonker's film is just how professional it looks. It doesn't look like a big-budgeted Hollywood film, but it does look about a million times nicer than most of the shot-on-video and digital stuff that's so popular in goredom. The decision to use actual film really adds an air of professionalism to the production—making it play like a legitimate film—which is something that's totally missing in 99% of the shot-on-video movies out there.

***Darkness'*** look is also aided by Jonker's directorial talents. I'm absolutely stunned (in a sad way) that this guy hasn't made another film. ***Darkness*** is rough (it's not as polished as Tobe Hooper's ***Texas Chainsaw Massacre***, but for comparison purposes, those two films fit together nicely) but it's hard to miss the fact that Jonker has some genuine talent—and that with a bigger budget, real actors, and someone to help with the screenwriting duties, he could have been a legitimate talent.

In fact, most of the faults of **Darkness** stem from the lack of a budget. Take, for example, the film's lack of proper lighting in most of the night sequences (rarely has a title been more fitting for a film...), the bad acting (there's not a legitimate actor in the entire cast, most of the performers were teenagers from the local high school drama club), and less than stellar dialogue and over reliance on narration (things that a more polished scriptwriter would have fixed)—all of these things seem to spring almost directly from a lack of cash. Given money, and some guidance, Jonker could probably make one hell of a film. That **Darkness** is accomplished as it is is an amazing feat when you look at what he was up against.

But, enough of that—let's talk about the gore.

**Darkness** delivers the red stuff in copious amounts throughout its roughly 90-minute running time. The film's effects platter is a veritable smorgasbord of gore featuring gunshots to the head, chainsaw massacres, ripped out throats, and a vampire meltdown at the climax that features enough fake blood to fill a swimming pool. If you're not impressed, then you're even more jaded than I am.

Whatever the case, **Leif Jonker's Darkness** is a great little splatter film. It's nice to see vampire carnage instead of the more traditional zombies, and it's even nicer to see a low budget movie that's actually shot on film. The real shame of **Darkness** is that it seems to be the only film that Jonker will ever make—which is sad, since he shows a huge amount of potential in his debut production.

# CHAPTER THIRTY-FOUR

# MANIAC (1980)

**Directed by: William Lustig**

**Barf Bag Rating:**

I WARNED YOU
NOT TO GO OUT
TONIGHT
MANIAC
"Maniac" Starring Joe Spinell  Caroline Munro
Produced by Andrew Garroni and William Lustig  Directed by William Lustig
DOLBY STEREO
ANALYSIS FILM CORPORATION
A NEW FILM DISTRIBUTION COMPANY

Here's another classic that many mainstream horror film fans have never seen. Released in 1980, William Lustig's *Maniac* was met with both a critical drubbing and condemnation by various groups for both its misogynistic undertone and its excessive gore effects. *Maniac* is definitely a violent and gory film, an exploitation classic to be sure, but it's also quite compelling. Its bleak worldview, its decision to show the film from the killer's point of view, and its decidedly low-budget feel all work to make *Maniac* play like a precursor to another low-budget classic—John McNaughton's *Henry: Portrait of a Serial Killer*. And while Lustig's film isn't quite as good as McNaughton's, fans of *Henry* should find things to like in *Maniac*.

The film, which drew at least some of its inspiration from the Son of Sam murders, centers on Frank Zito (Joe Spinell) a greasy, grimy man (who bears more than a bit of a resemblance to porn film legend Ron Jeremy) who was abused by his mother as a child. As a result of this abuse, Frank has some major resentment issues toward women—ones he deals with by stalking and murdering them, then cutting off their scalps as souvenirs. He takes the scalps back to his dingy little apartment (along with their clothes) and dresses female mannequins in his victim's belongings.

Zito is haunted by his actions—and like most compulsions, he seems powerless to stop them despite the fact that he realizes what he's doing is wrong. Eventually, he meets a young female photographer, Anna (Caroline Munro), and it appears as if he's going to get himself under control. But alas, it's not to be, as the film reaches its gruesome climax with Zito back to his old tricks.

*Maniac* is a gritty film that benefits from some deft direction by Lustig as well as a tour de force performance from Spinell. While Lustig's direction is never flashy or flamboyant, he does a fine job of capturing the seedy underbelly of NYC. There's a grimness in every frame of this film, even the ones that are supposed to be in nice places—one that adds immeasurably to the overall effect of the movie. Couple that with the sleazy performance from Spinell, and you'll find yourself wanting to take a shower after watching this movie.

And what of Spinell's performance? It's right up there with Michael Rooker's portrayal of Henry Lee Lucas. Spinell *is* Frank Zito...a savage murderer who you can't help but feel bad for in some of the scenes. Yes, Zito is a madman, but he's also a madman who was made that way through prior abuse. The film never attempts to condone the actions of the character, but it does present him in a light where you can feel a little sympathy for him—something that makes the film even more disturbing. Spinell has done the nearly impossible here—creating a three-dimensional monster.

Surprisingly, *Maniac* even has some scares to it. One long sequence deals with Spinell stalking a young nurse through an abandoned subway station. The tension is set to fever pitch as she chooses to hide in an empty stall in the women's restroom—while Spinell works his way ever closer. And while the end of the sequence isn't quite as graphic and frightening as what you were imaging it to be in the moments prior to it happening, it's still pretty disturbing stuff.

*Maniac* also features the special effects work of the legendary Tom Savini. Savini's efforts here are top notch...the scalpings look good, and the climactic sequence is a great setup foreshadowing a set-piece that he would eventually use in *Day of the Dead*. However, this film is infamous with the gore crowd for one reason—the shotgun blast to the head effect.

Savini sets up a scene where he and a young woman make out in the backseat of a car. The woman sees Frank watching them, and begs Savini to take her home. He complies, but when he turns on his headlights, Frank's standing directly in front of them. Frank then jumps on the hood of the car, raises a shotgun, and shoots Savini in the face, through the windshield. Savini's head literally explodes in a shower of blood, gore, and bone fragments. It's incredibly gruesome, even edging out the exploding head in Cronenberg's *Scanners*. And now, twenty years later, in an era of space-age special effects, it's still the standard by which all exploding head gore effects are judged. *Maniac* is worth seeing for this scene alone.

Despite all these positives, *Maniac* remains something of a flawed film. The script (which Spinell co-wrote) becomes totally unfocused by the last act. The entire Frank/Anna love angle feels like an afterthought to pad the runtime. The other problem with the love story is that it takes quite a bit of willing suspension of disbelief to accept that the lovely Munro would ever even talk to the grimy Zito, let alone date him.

Lustig and Spinell had plans to make a sequel to **Maniac** (even going as far as to shoot a trailer for it) but they couldn't ever find financial backing for the film, and then Spinell died of a heart attack in 1989. The trailer for **Maniac 2** is out there if you're curious about what might have been. The film was also remade in 2012 (with Elijah Wood in the lead role), but that version isn't quite as much fun as the original.

**Maniac** will never be mistaken for art—it's a film that revels in its sleaziness and has no other ambitions than to entertain and disturb its audience. While it is a mean little film, one that most viewers will find too gritty and stark to actually like, it's still one of the standout titles in the slasher, gore, and exploitation canons. If you're into any of the aforementioned genres, then **Maniac** belongs in your video collection.

# CHAPTER THIRTY-FIVE

# NEW YORK RIPPER (1982)

Directed by: Lucio Fulci

**Barf Bag Rating:**

Alternate titles: *Squartatore di New York, Lo; Psycho Ripper (1982); Ripper, The (1982)*

LO SQUARTATORE DI NEW YORK
JACK HEDLEY · ALMANTA KELLER · HOWARD ROSS · ANDREW PAINTER
ALEXANDRA DELLI COLLI   e con la partecipazione di PAOLO MALCO   Regia di LUCIO FULCI
Prodotto dalla FULVIA FILM s.r.l.-ROMA   Colore LV di LUCIANO VITTORI

In the opening scene of Lucio Fulci's 1982 giallo/slasher flick, ***New York Ripper***, the astute Fulci fan is treated to several of the legendary Italian goremeister's cinematic trademarks. In a deserted New York lot, with the Brooklyn Bridge looming in the background, a man plays fetch with his dog. He throws the stick into some dense foliage and we watch, in a long shot, as the dog brings his bounty back to his master. We never see just what the dog has brought back, but Fulci gives us one of his infamous cut shots to the man's face—then zooms in so that only his eyes are visible. From this expression, we know something's not right. Then, with a discordant blast of music designed to jangle our nerves, he cuts to the dog's mouth, then zooms in what it's carrying—a decomposing hand. Fulci holds the shot for several seconds, leering at the gore effect and allowing the audience to check it out in detail, then he cuts to another scene entirely.

For anyone who has seen more than three Fulci films (and paid attention), this opening sequence is indicative of his entire body of work as a filmmaker. There's an aesthetic at work in Fulci's films—an occasionally crass one that seems to revel in showing us gruesome things for longer than necessary, yet an aesthetic none the less.

It also demonstrates that other Fulci staple, a fascination with human eyes—and, eventually, the destruction of human eyes. However, while all of Fulci's films are gory (he wasn't dubbed the "godfather of gore" by fans for nothing), many of them were supernaturally tinged movies filled with zombies, which gave the films in question an almost comic book feel. It's hard to take the gore in a film like ***Zombie*** or ***City of the Living Dead*** in a serious way—zombies aren't real. But, ***New York Ripper*** was something of a departure for Fulci...a sleazy and overtly violent film very much grounded in reality. And it is at least partially because of this change in tone and the new direction (away from the more comic book-styled gore films) that this film is reviled by even many of Fulci's staunchest supporters. Of course, it's also why some of us champion it as one of his best films as well.

The story here is a simple one—a maniacal slasher is hacking up women in New York City. Detective Fred Williams (Jack Hedley) is trying to stop the madman before he can strike again. When the killer starts calling Williams personally (speaking in an oddly menacing Donald Duck voice, complete with quacks), the detective turns to college professor Paul Davis for insight. What ensues is a cat and mouse game as the cops hunt for the killer and try to keep the one victim to survive a ripper attack (Antonella Interlenghi's Fay Majors) alive.

Like all good gialli, **New York Ripper** is an elaborately crafted mystery filled with red herrings throughout its narrative. Nearly everyone is a suspect here at one point or another—and some folks are suspects more than once. The plotting of Fulci's films has never been one of the filmmaker's strong points, but here, there's actually something of a story to follow along with (which is reminiscent of his earlier giallo, e.g. **Don't Torture a Duckling**).

Of course, mystery elements alone do not a good giallo make. No, the gialli are just as infamous for their violent death—something that **New York Ripper** delivers in spades.

The violence and death in this film is stark and brutal—women are gutted from groin to sternum, one has a broken bottle rammed into her vagina, another has her nipple, then her eye, slowly bisected by a razor blade. Critics often site this film in particular when trying to label Fulci as a misogynistic woman hater—but I'm not sure that it's a legitimate point. Fulci always made violent films—and he always pushed the envelope in terms of gore. It just so happens that in this particular film, the killer chose to murder women. At any rate, philosophical arguments about the late Fulci's character aside, this film is one that should please any gore fan (although, a few of the props look a bit dated).

As mentioned above, the film has a really sleazy feel to it, featuring more sex and nudity than any other Fulci film I can recall. One scene takes place in a 42$^{nd}$ Avenue strip club, where a man and woman engage in live sex on stage in front of an audience. Another has a nymphomaniacal woman (Alexandra Delli Colli) being accosted by two men in a pool hall (which she clearly ends up enjoying). Later, she partakes in some bondage—with a man who may well be the ripper himself. At any rate, the sex scenes aren't the hardcore porn variety, but they are more than fans are used to seeing in Fulci's regular work.

In the opening paragraph, I talked about a few of the Fulci "trademarks"—which are essentially techniques that re-occurred in all of his films, often repeatedly. They've almost become visual cliché in a way—such was Fulci's over-reliance on these camera movements and shots. However, here in this film, after that first scene, we really don't see any of these visual elements again. Fulci makes one of his most impressive movies here, with several scenes actually showcasing assured camera movement. One scene in particular, a conversation between three or four people, features not only some smooth cuts from one person to the next, but also two nice rack focuses in one shot. Still, in spite of this improved directorial style, we still get a lot of leering long takes on any gore effect featured in the film. There's no implied violence here—Fulci gives it to us in full detail. Of course, in a scene like the eyeball slicing one (which readily brings to mind Bunuel's ***Un chien andalou***) this is something of an asset—mainly because the FX technician managed to get the eyeball to roll in the socket while the razor was cutting it—a very realistic shot.

Also worth noting is the improved editing. Some of Fulci's films (most notably ***City of the Living Dead***) were filled with jarring cuts from one scene to the next (cuts so jagged that they often nipped off the soundtrack in mid-note). Here, the transitions from one scene to the next are smooth, and the soundtrack is never cut off at the switch.

Speaking of the soundtrack, a lot of criticism has been leveled against the score of ***New York Ripper***--it's a weird blend of disco and jazz. However, considering the time period this film was made in, it fits. And, personally, I found it kind of groovy in a campy sort of way.

The acting is essentially what you'd expect in a low budget Italian slasher flick. Jack Hedley does a great job as the grizzled and clichéd police detective, though. Astute viewers will notice that Lucio Fulci himself turns up as a police captain early in the film.

***New York Ripper*** is easily the most reviled of Fulci's films overall. The relentlessly brutal story coupled with the graphic gore is disturbing, but faulting a horror filmmaker for making a movie that's upsetting and violent seems to be at least somewhat misguided. Fulci's job as a filmmaker has always been to get under an audience's skin—and I think here he achieves that desired effect more effectively than in almost any of his other films. Like any Fulci flick, this one has some problems (most notably the somewhat absurd motivation for the killer's action at the climax), but it also features some of the director's most competent filmmaking. If you fancy yourself a Fulci fan, admirer of Euro-horror, or exploitation film lover, then ***New York Ripper*** belongs in your video library. It's a sleazy, gore-filled classic.

# NIKOS THE IMPALER (2003)

**Director: Andreas Schnaas**

**Barf Bag Rating:**

Alternate titles: *Nikos; Violent Shit 4: Nikos*

INCLUDES EXTRA BONUS MATERIALS
NIKOS
THE IMPALER
THE BIG APPLE
GETS A NEW
IMMIGRANT
AND A VERY
BIG PROBLEM!
"ONE OF THE GORIEST FILMS
OF THE YEAR" – Fangoria
DVD
VIDEO
18

German goremeister Andreas Schnaas is back in action with ***Nikos the Impaler***—yet another low-budget splatter epic that may well be his best film.

Schnaas plays Nikos, a Romanian warlord killed in the Middle Ages. When a modern day art thief bleeds on his ancient war mask, the barbarian is resurrected in New York City circa 2003 with one thing on his mind—killing everything that moves.

After slashing his way through the art gallery and its collection of smarmy critics and slacker college kids, Nikos hits the streets of the Big Apple—and much carnage ensues. Playing as a riff on both Lamberto Bava's ***Demons*** and Rob Hedden's ***Friday the 13th Part VIII: Jason Takes Manhattan***, it's never quite as good as former, but infinitely more fun than the latter.

While decidedly low-budget in appearance, the film looks light years better than anything else Schnaas has filmed up to this point. Visually, the film has its problems (most notably a matting issue that has the top of the frame decapitating actors in more than a few scenes as well as some lighting problems that make some scenes too dark in the print I saw for this review), but Schnaas and crew more than make up for their lack of polished filmmaking skills with their sheer exuberance for the material. Anyone looking to a film called ***Nikos the Impaler*** for brilliant acting, amazing direction, or a musing on the role of Romania in the post-communist world would be advised to look elsewhere—gorehounds seeking a great time with lots of mindless splatter effects and cheesy production values will be in heaven.

Utilizing an ensemble cast, the performances in ***Nikos*** are hit-and-miss. Leads Joe Zaso and Felissa Rose (who observant splatterphiles will remember from ***Sleepaway Camp***) are actually decent. Schnaas takes the relatively simple role of Nikos and manages to almost screw it up with some hammy gesticulations and way too much grunting. In many ways, Nikos isn't a whole lot different than Schnaas' Karl the Butcher character from his earlier ***Violent Shit*** films. Still, while he's no Kane Hodder, there's a certain amount of endearing charm in the way Schnaas plays Nikos—it's almost comedic, and I get the impression that it was intentional.

Nikos is an equal-opportunity impaler—the guy kills everyone: senior citizens, cops, a naked Darian Caine, Troma film producers and stars (Lloyd Kaufman and Debbie Rochon in cameo appearances), college kids, art critics, security guards, fans viewing a double feature of earlier Schnaas films, and even Adolf Hitler! After a relatively slow opening act, the blood flows fast and furious for the rest of the film. No one is safe from Nikos.

Of course, the climax is a bit underwhelming—Nikos "resurrects" Hitler, a succubus, a zombie, and two ninjas using some sort of weird wizardry skills on a few video cassette covers. Naturally, when Der Fuhrer (who looks like he's been hitting the donuts pretty hard while spending eternity in Hell) can't acquiesce to Nikos being the leader of the group, he gets killed anyway. Unfortunately, Nikos' demise isn't nearly as gory as the rest of the film—a definite downer as well.

Jesus Vega and Marcus Koch's special effects work is solid throughout. Nikos' weapon of choice is his huge sword (which looks like it was made out of painted plywood) and he beheads, disembowels, and dismembers more people than I could count with it. When he gets tired of that, he can throw spears, kill people with free weights, rip them in half with his bare hands, and kill with pretty much any environmental object he happens to stumble across. The gore is plentiful and looks good despite the budget restraints—meaning there's no shortage of animal intestines and stringy latex on display here.

While no one's ever gonna mistake Andreas Schnaas for Orson Welles, I thank god every day for guys like him and Olaf Ittenbach. While the films of these German gore auteurs may not be "great cinema" in the traditional sense of the phrase, they're still pretty damn entertaining. And at the end of the day, entertaining an audience is what movies are all about.

# CHAPTER THIRTY-SEVEN

# PIECES (1982)

**Directed by: Juan Piquer Simon**

**Barf Bag Rating:**

YOU DON'T HAVE TO GO TO TEXAS
FOR A CHAINSAW MASSACRE!
ABSOLUTELY NO ONE UNDER 17 ADMITTED TO THIS PERFORMANCE
PIECES
IT'S EXACTLY WHAT YOU THINK IT IS!
Starring CHRISTOPHER GEORGE PAUL SMITH
EDMUND PURDOM LINDA DAY Music by CAM
Screenplay by DICK RANDALL & JOHN SHADOW
Produced by DICK RANDALL & STEVE MANASIAN Directed by J. SIMON

Nostalgia can be a funny thing--it has this knack for making things that were decent seem a lot better in retrospect. This is particularly true when it comes to movies. I'm sure all of us can remember at least one film we loved as a kid--and when we saw it as an adult, our reaction to it was invariably completely opposite. Over the course of the past few years, I've noticed this particular phenomenon applies really well to horror films--something that scared the bejesus out of us as a kid rarely has any affect at all on our adult selves. What was graphically gory in childhood often looks pretty tame today.

Rare is the film that holds up to our memory of it from all those years ago--and I went into Juan Piquer Simon's 1982 slasher film *Pieces* expecting it to be nowhere near as cool as I remembered it. I was wrong.

*Pieces* is one of those films that really evokes memories of the golden days of slasher movies. It's sleazy, violent, politically incorrect to a fault, and mostly nonsensical.

The '80s were an era of excess, so it's only fitting that horror cinema from that period should ape those same values--which is something *Pieces* does quite brilliantly. Don't get me wrong--this isn't a great piece of cinema. It is, however, one of the more entertaining and audacious slasher films from the early days of the form.

Opening in the past, viewers watch as a young boy puts together a jigsaw puzzle. Rather than being a scenic vista or a photo of some cartoon character, we soon learn that the image is a fully naked woman. Mom bursts in, sees the puzzle, and flips out. Junior then axes her in the head, hides in the closet, and fools the cops into thinking he was an innocent bystander when they arrive.

Jump forward a bunch of years and our psychotic killer is now frequenting a university. Armed with a chainsaw and a burning desire to create his own naked woman jigsaw puzzle out of female body parts, he slices through the student body.

Lieutenant Bracken (and yes, this movie gets style points for giving the main character my last name and having stalwart Christopher George tackle the role) is on the case, along with female inspector Mary Riggs (George's real life wife

Lynda Day George), Sgt. Holden (Frank Brana), and a student (Ian Sera). Can this intrepid team stop the demented madman before he completes his grisly task? What do you think?

Co-written by Italian sleaze auteur Joe D'Amato (credited as John Shadow on some prints), **Pieces** is a film that's often short on logic but filled to the brim with sleaze and gore. When our maniacal slasher isn't stalking and killing some hapless coed (watch as one wets herself in close-up before meeting her demise), D'Amato's got some other girl running around topless for no good reason. They don't make 'em like this anymore--and that's sort of a shame. The script does take a lame stab at giallo-esque mystery with the killer's identity, but the red-herring is so obviously a McGuffin that no one buys it anyway and everyone can pretty much guess who the real murderer is.

The acting is of the "ham and cheese" variety. Lynda Day George is wonderfully awful (as usual), particularly in one scene where she screams "bastard" four times in frustration at her own inability to stop the killer. Don't sweat it, Lynda--no one really thinks you're gonna crack the case--you're just here to be eye candy.

Edmund Purdom and Paul Smith deserve special recognition for going well above and beyond the call of duty in the scenery-chewing department as well. Of the cast, only Christopher George can actually act--and he spends most of the film looking bewildered, like he wonders just how his career reached a point where he has to take work in movies like this.

The film is incredibly stupid in parts (watch for the kung-fu guy's scene—that was Dick Randall's attempt to promote one of his knockoff Bruce Le movies) and has more plot holes than there are craters on the moon. But, every time you get ready to throw in the towel, Simon comes along with another stalk-and-kill sequence.

For those of you who were disappointed that Texas Chainsaw Massacre didn't really have any chainsaw gore in it, this film is for you. Simon revels in the chainsaw slaughter, and the end result is one of the more gruesome slasher films of the period. Rest assured, no one was aiming for a PG rating with this one.

When you get right down to it, ***Pieces*** is a product of its time--an era when slasher films were still relatively new, when filmmakers got away with a lot more violence and sleaze, and when Euro-horror was in its prime. Watching the film is a lot like opening a time capsule back to those days--and surprisingly enough, this particular film is just as good, gory, and sleazy as I remembered it. Nostalgia may often make things seem better in retrospect than they really were, but Pieces bucks that trend.

# CHAPTER THIRTY-EIGHT

# PLAGA ZOMBIE: THE MUTANT ZONE (2001)

Directed by: Pablo Pares and Hernan Saez

**Barf Bag Rating:**

PERDIERON UNA BATALLA,
PERO LA GUERRA CONTINÚA.
LIMITE DE
LA CIUDAD
PLAGA ZOMBIE
ZONA MUTANTE

If we've learned anything during this little excursion into the bowels of gore cinema, it's that no one country has a lock on the creation of disgusting movies. Earlier entries have come from all corners of the globe. However, **Plaga Zombie: Mutant Zone** may be the only gore film to ever emanate from Argentina. That alone makes it the best, but I've got a feeling that even if there were some competition for the title, this little film would still wear the crown.

Written, directed, and starring Pablo Pares, Hernan Saez, and Berta Muniz, it becomes obvious early on that this is a labor of love created by three guys who grew up with on a steady diet of Sam Raimi and Peter Jackson films. Pares is Bill Johnson, a med student. Saez is Max Giggs, a techno-geek. Muniz is John West, a down-on-his-luck professional wrestler. No, I'm not making this up.

Together, our three heroes find themselves trapped in a city overrun by the undead. It seems that an alien life force has bribed officials into allowing them to do an experiment on the locals—only the experiment turns the citizens into bloodthirsty monsters and eventually spreads well beyond the agreed upon area. Johnson and company are tossed directly into the hot zone and must escape the city before the zombies devour them—all while dodging FBI agents and various other bands of survivors.

As you can see, the story isn't anything spectacular or groundbreaking. What really sets **Plaga Zombie: Mutant Zone** apart from the rest of the pack is just how good it looks (since it was made on a budget that probably would have paid for a nice lunch here in America) and how amazing the gore work is.

Watching **Plaga Zombie**, it's hard not to think of Robert Rodriguez's **El Mariachi**—another south of the border production made for a few pesos that looks far better than a lot of movies with 100 times the budget. Granted, **Plaga Zombie** doesn't have the same level of shine as Rodriguez's flick (but then again, that film was cleaned up for a wide release by Columbia Pictures) but what these guys have accomplished with so little money is truly spectacular. The gore work alone leads one to think these guys were working with a much larger budget.

And while the gore is the unmitigated star of the film, **Plaga Zombie** also features three fine performances from its main cast members. All three leads are interesting, but it's Berta Muniz as wrestler John West who steals the show. Muniz hams it up with professional wrestler style throughout, and he even has his own badass theme song (which has been stuck in my head for days now). Muniz carries the film on his not inconsiderable shoulders whenever things slow down and it threatens to derail. This is a cult classic character—not unlike Bruce Campbell's Ash or Lionel in Jackson's ***Dead Alive***.

The gore work itself is suitably gross, complete with beheadings, spurting blood (and other bodily fluids), full body dismemberment, intestinal rope, and more. This is a gore fan's dream production, and the effects work definitely stands up to serious scrutiny.

If all of the above weren't clear enough, I'm now a huge fan of ***Plaga Zombie: Mutant Zone***. This is a film made for fans of gore cinema by fans of gore cinema and that love shines through in each and every scene. This is a film that should be seen by fans of extreme cult cinema, then talked about so other fans don't miss it. It's not a perfect film, but it does so many things right that it's hard to hold its faults against it.

Viva John West!

# CHAPTER THIRTY-NINE

# PREMUTOS (1997)

**Directed by: Olaf Ittenbach**

**Barf Bag Rating:**

Alternate titles: *Premutos - Der gefallene Engel; Premutos: Lord of the Living Dead (1997) (USA: video title); Premutos: The Fallen Angel (1997) (International: literal title English title)*

2-DISC EXTENDED DIRECTOR'S CUT
OLAF ITTENBACH'S
PREMUTOS
THE FALLEN ANGEL
UNEARTHED CLASSICS

*__I won't let you spoil my party—even if it sucks big time!--Walter,__*
*__Premutos__*

To truly appreciate Olaf Ittenbach's **Premutos** one must view it as what it was meant to be—a love letter to fans of gore cinema. Ittenbach has little interest in the things that traditionally make cinema good—acting, direction, the screenplay, etc.—and instead spends the majority of his time focusing on the gory set-pieces he's so gleefully created. Because of this, **Premutos** has a very niche audience—people who love films like **Evil Dead** and Peter Jackson's **Dead Alive**. If you fall into that camp, run out and find a copy as soon as possible—Ittenbach made this film specifically for you. If you don't enjoy the aforementioned films, you'll want to stay far, far away from **Premutos**.

What little story there is in the film deals with Premutos, the first fallen angel, one who even predates Lucifer. Premutos has spent thousands of years wandering the Earth while trying to destroy humanity. He takes human form as a kid named Mathias (none other than director Ittenbach), who seems to die a gruesome John Morghen-styled death every couple of decades.

However, things are going to be different this time around as Premutos finally succeeds in taking his true form while at his stepfather's birthday party. Freed of his human shell, and armed with a small army of the undead, Premutos sets out for world domination.

Truthfully, from a technical filmmaking standpoint, **Premutos** is pretty awful. It's got a miniscule budget (and it shows—repeatedly), Ittenbach's script is dreadful (the dinner party sequence is unbearably long and painful to watch), the direction is amateurish at best, and the actors, for the most part, all suck (I did love Christopher Stacey as Walter though—this guy could have joined the ranks of Ash and Reggie from **Phantasm** as far as everyman horror heroes go).

So, what makes **Premutos** worth watching? Simply put, the gore. Ittenbach has clearly been inspired by both Sam Raimi (one character even has an **Evil Dead** poster on the wall in her room) and Peter Jackson. While he lacks the technical skill level of either director, he more than makes up for it with his youthful exuberance. Unlike his countryman and fellow gore filmmaker Andreas Schnaas,

Ittenbach's films do have at least some polish to them. This also makes **Premutos** pretty enjoyable.

The Raimi/Jackson influence is notable in almost every frame of the film, but several really drive the point home. A shot from the perspective of a flying ashtray is so patently from the Raimi and Scott Spiegel school that it almost borders on plagiarism. Meanwhile, a scene with a character picking his nose, rolling the booger into a ball, and flicking it across the room directly into the open mouth of his snooty girlfriend is something straight out of a Jackson film.

The film's pace flags badly during the second act, where Ittenbach spends way too much time showing us a dreadful dinner party, but those who tough it out will be rewarded by the film's final act—an all out orgy of gore and violence.

The climax of **Premutos** certainly gives **Dead Alive** a run for its money in terms of pure carnage and sheer audacity. There's nothing quite as inventive as Lionel taking out wave after wave of zombies with the deck of a lawnmower, but the level of gore and the number of dead is roughly equal. As far as climaxes go, **Premutos**, like **Dead Alive** and John Woo's **Hard Boiled**, leaves the viewer exhausted at its conclusion.

Finally, I'd be shirking my duties if I didn't mention the ultimate means of victory for Hugo and crew. While I've always said that the helicopter crashing through the roof of the Metropol theater in Lamberto Bava's **Demons** was the greatest deus ex machina ending in horror cinema, I think Ittnebach has finally outdone it. Somehow, Hugo finds a tank—and can drive it—to deal with the zombies once and for all.

While Olaf Ittnebach is not a filmmaker for the masses, it's easy to see why gorehounds revere his work. While his reach often exceeds the grasp of his talent and budget, there's no denying the enthusiasm he brings to his work. Ittenbach loves splatter—and he makes no apologies for it. I think we can all admire that. I'd prefer to watch a bad movie made by a passionate filmmaker than a competently-lensed big budget production with absolutely no soul. **Premutos** has heart—and it's not afraid to show it to you as its characters rip it right out of your chest.

# CHAPTER FORTY

# SLAUGHTERED VOMIT DOLLS (2006)

**Directed by: Lucifer Valentine**

**Barf Bag Rating: 5**

Slaughtered omit dolls
starring: Ameara LaVey
R.I.P. Angela
directed by: Lucifer Valentine 666
blacklava entertainment
© kingdom of hell productions inc.

During my years as a fan and critic of extreme cinema, I've seen a lot of screwed up shit. I've seen special effects-created death from the finest practitioners of the form, real autopsy footage, countless genuine deaths in mondo videos, and even more than a few fetish porn titles. I'm essentially jaded when it comes to this stuff--it's hard to shock me. ***Slaughtered Vomit Dolls***, though, is one of the few films that actually affected me--so much so that I wound up feeling a little nauseous at a few points. If that doesn't convince you just how truly messed up this "movie" is, then I don't know what will...other than seeing it for yourself.

The brainchild of director Lucifer Valentine, ***Slaughtered Vomit Dolls*** is one of the most divisive films in the annals of gross out cinema. About half the people who see it come away from it amazed by how well-crafted and repellant it is, while the other half finds it to be complete garbage. This second half often likes to say that they also didn't find it all that graphic or disturbing. That scares me a bit--you may not like ***Slaughtered Vomit Dolls***, but I don't think you can realistically make a case for it not being absolutely one of the sickest films ever put to tape. Sure, if I'd shelled out $35 for it I might be a little disappointed with the end result, but if you saw it and honestly found nothing disturbing about it, you're into a whole other realm of hardcore.

Honestly, ***Slaughtered Vomit Dolls*** isn't so much a film as it is an endurance test. It's a grindhouse experiment in seeing how much a viewer can take, a YouTube postcard sent from the very bowels of Hell. Whether it's good or not is almost irrelevant--it doesn't really exist to be "good" or "bad." Instead, it mostly just exists to gross people out, and in that regard it's successful.

Ameara LaVey plays Blisters, a bulimic runaway stripper-prostitute who pledges her life to Satan. What follows is open to interpretation--it could be hallucinations, or it could be something else entirely. Either way, viewers are treated to a series of sequences where someone brutally murders a group of young women. One has her eyeballs stabbed repeatedly then ripped out. Another has her face peeled off. A third, who says she's a recovering bulimic, has her arm chopped off--then in a strange bit of dark humor, her assailant gives her a guitar that she can't play. Yet another victim has the top of his head sawed off, his brain eaten, then his assailant regurgitates it back into his empty cranium.

If that weren't enough, we haven't even covered the copious barfing that gives **Slaughtered Vomit Dolls** its name. I'll admit that I have a bit of a weakness when it comes to people ralphing. I can take a little puking, sure--I'm not one of those people who immediately tosses his cookies when someone else does. However, some of the vomiting scenes in this film last for five minutes or more (easily outdoing the puking scene in Shozin Fukui's **964 Pinocchio**, which was sort of the world record holder in this dubious category) and listening to/watching someone lose their lunch for that long is bound to make just about anyone queasy.

This isn't even taking the film's coup de grace into consideration, a lengthy segment where a man named Henry uses a severed arm to gag himself, then spews his stomach contents all over the camera and everything else in the room. He follows this up by ralphing in a big glass and drinking it down-one of the few times in my life where I actually looked at a film and said "you've got to be fucking kidding me..." It's gross--which is why its inclusion here was a no brainer

Yet, unlike so many gore films (which are often exercises in just being gross for the sake of being gross), there's some legitimate talent on display here.

Visually, the film has a lot of static scenes, which could become really boring, but Valentine keeps things interesting by blurring the frame, inserting tons of weird cuts, and using the static set-up from various parts of the same room. Audio-wise, the film keeps things ominous by playing lots of music and dialogue backwards, slowing down the audio track so people sound more evil, and using music that's more jarring than melodic. Granted, all of these effects are overused throughout **Slaughtered Vomit Dolls'** 70-minute running time, but Valentine shows lot of potential here (potential that's realized in the film's two sequels). Of course, if you find any kind of arthouse-style filmmaking annoying, then a lot of this movie is going to bother you.

I still don't really know how I feel about **Slaughtered Vomit Dolls**, but I do know that it affected me as a viewer--and any film evokes a response from me (other than apathy, maybe) is at least a success on some level. The movie isn't the goriest around, and there's certainly been grosser vomiting in some of the Japanese fetish videos out there, but the way Valentine has combined gore and vomit with a unique visual and audio style certainly makes ***Slaughtered Vomit Dolls*** something more than just your standard extreme genre film. Love it or hate it, if you truly think you're a hardcore gorehound then you need to see this film.

# SPLATTER: NAKED BLOOD (1995)

**Directed by: Hisayasu Sato**

**Barf Bag Rating:**

Alternate titles: *Megyaku: Akuma no yorokobi; Itainoga suki (1995) (V) (Japan: subtitle); Naked Blood (1995) (V)*

SPLATTER:
NAKED
BLOOD

If we've learned one thing in the course of this little tome, it's that gore cinema may have started in America and been perfected by the Italians, but the Japanese make some of the sickest movies ever committed to celluloid (or, in some cases, video). For further proof of this (as if the **Guinea Pig** movies weren't enough) one need look no further than Hisayasu Sato's 1995 film **Splatter: Naked Blood**.

**Splatter** is the feel good tale of Eiji (Sadao Abe) a young wannabe scientist. Like America's own Doogie Howser, Eiji's something of a prodigy—we know this because he writes lots of notes in his little PC diary. Eiji's current cause is to eliminate all human pain and suffering. He's concluded that his drug, called Myson, can cause a massive rush of endorphins from the human brain whenever the body feels pain—thus turning the pain into pleasure. Unfortunately, our underage Einstein isn't worldly enough to realize that turning pain into pleasure is what makes masochists tick, but more on that later...

Armed with his new drug (which looks suspiciously like Windex), Eiji sets out to find guinea pigs for experimentation. It just so turns out that his mother is also a scientist, and she's working on a new contraceptive drug. Eiji slips the Myson into the IV bags with the contraceptive, and watches from a distance as three nubile young Japanese girls (are there any other kind in these films?) are injected with his new wonder drug.

The three girls are all pretty one-dimensional, save for lead female Rika (Misa Aika). Rika informs us that she doesn't sleep—she's the lucky one in a million person who loses the need for rest when she gets her first menstrual cycle. Because of this, she lives in an apartment with a giant cactus that's hooked up to a biofeedback machine, and she can hear plants talking. Rika is just the kind of girl you want to take home to mom.

Her two new friends are even less developed—one is obsessed with the pleasures of food, while the other agonizes over her appearance. Give yourself a screenwriter's credit if you can figure out how this vital information is going to play into these young women's' demise....

Eiji follows the three around in order to see how they're reacting to the Myson—and it isn't good. The food girl is slowly devouring herself in a fit of ecstasy, while our model wannabe has taken to extreme body modification by piercing. Eiji flips out, not only because the drug isn't working in quite the way he imagined, but also because he's now in love with Rika—and she's had the drug, too, meaning she's probably gonna start doing weird stuff any minute now...

There's even more to the plot (which is quite involved for a splatter film, honestly), including a weird Oedipal scene, the return of Eiji's lost father, and a twist ending that's mildly amusing despite being relatively unnecessary.

However, the real reason most people check out **Splatter** is for the gore—and the film never disappoints in this regard. Aside from the infamous eye eating, viewers are treated to piercings, an evisceration, a sliced off nipple, sliced off vaginal lips (at least, they give the impression of being vaginal lips...we're never really sure), and a deep fried human hand. It takes awhile for the gore to show up, but it's definitely worth the wait.

Yet, to view **Splatter** as merely a gore film does a bit of disservice to the movie. While no one's going to be mistaking the film for art, it does offer up a far more impressive narrative than your standard gore offering. In fact, the idea behind the Myson drug is an interesting one that plays as potentially real. This adds another layer to a film could have worked solely as exploitation cinema.

Ultimately, though, it's the gorehounds who are gonna get the most out of **Splatter**. The effects work here is the real star of the show (people still marvel over the eye scene) and anyone looking for a gory good time would be well advised to track down a copy. While the MPAA has all but killed gore in America, and the Italian economy killed it in Italy, the Japanese are still doling out guts by the bucket-load.

# STORY OF RICKY, THE (1991)

**Directed by: Ngai Kai Lam**

**Barf Bag Rating:**

Alternate titles: *Riki-Oh; Lai Wong*

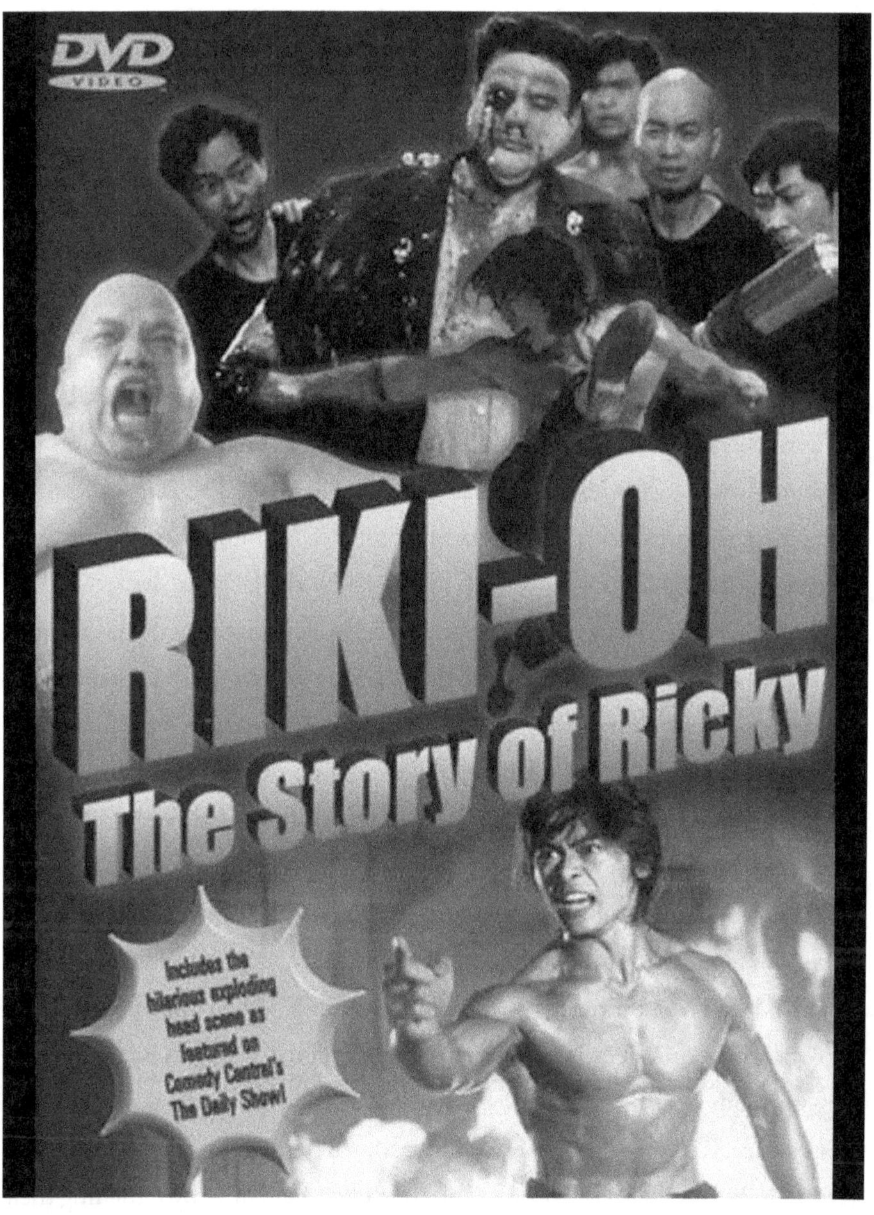
DVD
VIDEO
RIKI-OH
The Story of Ricky
Includes the
hilarious exploding
head scene as
featured on
Comedy Central's
The Daily Show!

As Peter Jackson has so deftly demonstrated, one doesn't need to make a horror film to make an effective gore flick. While gore and the inherent violence of horror films seem to go hand in hand, the comedic film also presents an almost limitless amount of opportunities for onscreen carnage—one just has to be a little more imaginative to find the right moments to splash the blood and guts across the screen. For proof of this, one need look no further than Jackson's **Bad Taste** and **Dead Alive**—classic examples of the gore comedy. Viewers who find those films to their liking will want be sure to track down a copy of Ngai Kai Lam's **The Story of Ricky**—another hilarious splatter epic that has to be seen to be believed.

Alternately titled **Riki-Oh**, **The Story of Ricky** is chop-socky masterpiece based on a wildly over-the-top Japanese manga. Siu Wong Fan stars as Ricky, a young martial artist given a ten-year prison sentence for murdering the guy who killed his girlfriend. Ricky's a badass, witnessed by the fact that he sets off the prison's metal detector because he kept the five bullets that his victim shot into him lodged in his chest as "souvenirs". In the future (which is not entirely unlike the present), prisons are run by private corporations—and the warden and the assistant warden at Ricky's prison don't like him one bit. Because of this, they'll torture Ricky continually—culminating in a never-ending sequence of atrocities once Ricky burns down their secret opium field.

Fear not for Ricky, though—he's a master of a special brand of kung-fu that allows him to punch through walls, tombstones, and when he feels like it (which is often), human bodies. The warden and the Gang of Four (four superthugs who essentially run the prison from the inside) will try to thwart Ricky at every turn—but our boyish Bruce Lee lookalike is more than up to the task.

In essence, Ricky is sort of like a Chinese Martin Luther King Jr.—if Dr. King settled his disputes with the people who were oppressing him by punching their heads off and ripping out their entrails. All Ricky wants is for his people (the other inmates) to be treated like human beings—The Man (in the form of the warden and his cronies) will have none of that, though—so Ricky has to step up and fight the power, becoming a hero and a leader to his people in the process. Or maybe not...

Putting those allegorical elements aside, *The Story of Ricky* works best when viewed as a wild thrill ride of gory excess. It's all but impossible to take this film too seriously—the assistant warden has a claw for a hand and a fake eyeball (filled with a seemingly never ending supply of breath mints), the effeminate Gang of Four leader is played by a woman (Yukari Oshima) in drag, and the violence is so off the wall that it's hard to imagine anyone being offended by it. If films like *August Underground* use gore to shock and repulse an audience, *The Story of Ricky* takes it and utilizes it as one more comedic gag.

This is not to say that the gore in the film is less effective for its slapstick tone—because it isn't. It's just that watching a serial killer hack up a corpse in his bathtub is a lot more "disturbing" than seeing a member of the Gang of Four crush a guy's head with his bare hands. Rather than eliciting the stunned silence of something like *Guinea Pig*, *The Story of Ricky* all but encourages its audience to hoot, holler, and "eww" at the onscreen bloodletting.

Gore fans will no doubt be pleased by the carnage on display—and highlighting all of it would take an entire review of its own. Highlights include the aforementioned head smash (which was a regular clip on *The Daily Show* with Craig Kilborn), a guy who eviscerates himself then tries to strangle our hero with his own intestines, razorblades in the mouth, numerous punched off heads, and in my favorite bit, Ricky's arm tendons are sliced by a knife—so he ties them back together and continues his fight. That's just good stuff.

*Story of Ricky* may not be the goriest film on display here, but it's one of the best starting points for the neophyte splatter fan. The humorous tone is a stark contrast to many of the more nihilistic gore films out there, which allows viewers to ease into the subgenre without jumping right off into the abyss with their first movie. Don't let the fact that it's lighthearted turn you off, though—there's enough gore, guts, and grue here to satisfy even the most jaded gorehound. *The Story of Ricky* is a splatter classic for a reason—it delivers the saucy stuff by the bucketful.

# CHAPTER FORTY-THREE

# STREET TRASH (1987)

**Director: Jim Muro**

**Barf Bag Rating:**

SPECIAL MELTDOWN EDITION
STREET TRASH
Synapse films

The guys at Mondo Digital called it "the greatest movie ever made about exploding bums!" and I'm inclined to agree with them. Of course, Jim Muro's 1987 gore classic *Street Trash* is also one of the only films I've ever seen that involved melting and exploding bums, but that's beside the point. What many critics and bewildered viewers have called nonsensical trash is a film that I call utterly classic...or something.

Ok, so *Street Trash* isn't a classic film by any stretch of the imagination. Hell, I'm not even sure it's all that good (but I think it is—and that's good enough for me). What I am sure of though, is that it's definitely top gore flicks of all time material. The story may be a disjointed mess of half-formed ideas with barely there characters in odd situations, but when it comes to the carnage, Muro and screenwriter Roy Frumkes deliver—in spades.

The film has sort of an Altman-esque quality to it, following around a series of hobos and ne'er-do-wells through a fictional city that seems to be comprised almost entirely of back alleys, dumps, and abandoned buildings. While mainstream films tend to make even the scuzziest characters and locales look at least somewhat clean, such is not the case in this film. *Street Trash* is the grimiest movie I've ever seen—I wanted to take a nice long bath after it was over. If nothing else, Muro deserves kudos for making a feature about bums with guys who look like real hobos and locations that would make Martha Stewart weep in sorrow.

Trying to explain the plot of *Street Trash* would require a book of its own, so let's just hit the highlights and be done with it. You're not watching this film for its classic three-act script structure anyway...

Mike Lackey plays Fred, a down-on-his-luck street person with a raging case of alcoholism. The owner of the local hooch emporium has discovered a case of some mysterious new rotgut called Viper hidden behind a wall. Not sure what the stuff is, he decides to sell it to the homeless community for a mere buck a bottle. What a guy—helping the homeless feed their addictions at an affordable price.

Unfortunately, there's something really wrong with Viper—drinking it causes the person doing the imbibing to ralph uncontrollably before melting into a pile of technicolored goo. Why does this happen? Who gives a crap—it's only here to provide ample opportunities for the effects crew to turn actors you've never seen before into piles of sludge. In this regard, it's a complete success.

When bums aren't drinking Viper and melting or exploding, there's like six different subplots running throughout the film. One has a grizzled cop (Bill Chepil) taking on Bronson (Vic Noto), the deranged king of the bums. We also watch a mafia subplot wherein the gangster's girlfriend is raped by a horde of homeless people, Chepil beat up a hitman and then puke all over him, necrophilia, an exploding hobo (stuffed with snack cakes from one of the film's few sponsors) and an engaging game of keep away involving a severed penis. Ah yes, **_Street Trash_** certainly delivers the goods.

And this delivery of the goods is what makes it so much fun despite the fact that nothing all that interesting happens for most of the first hour. The film has a definite "we have no clue what we're doing" vibe happening as the narrative flits from one plot element to the next like a crack addict with ADD. Couple this with a cast that ranges from community theater to B-movie level. Chepil and Lackey are particularly good, while most everyone else just hams it up to the best of their ability. Of course, much like the script, no one cares as long as the blood flows freely.

What is perhaps most interesting about **_Street Trash_** (aside from the gore, that is) is the direction of Jim Muro. This was Muro's debut feature and it's pretty spiffy in terms of camera movements. There's a lot of style, not unlike in the films of Scott Spiegel (of **_Intruder_** fame)—particularly in the use of the steadicam. What's fascinating about this is that Muro has since made a career for himself as a steadicam operator on films like **_Titanic_** and **_JFK_**. Too bad he couldn't have worked a few shots of exploding hobos into those movies.

Ultimately, **_Street Trash_** is a gore film for the sake of being a gore film. While the gore film can take many forms, this is it at its purest—designed solely to gross out an audience and make them hoot and holler at things that should make them extremely uncomfortable. While Muro's film doesn't have the passion of a Peter Jackson offering, it's certainly gross and entertaining and well worthy of being seen by any serious gore aficionado.

# CHAPTER FORTY-FOUR

# SUBCONSCIOUS CRUELTY (1999)

**Directed by: Karim Hussain**

**Barf Bag Rating:**

Subconscious
cruelty

Karim Hussain's ***Subconscious Cruelty*** opens with a ten-minute intro from the director himself. Normally, I'm not a fan of a director talking to the audience about his film before we view it—if the director needs to "explain" the film to me before I even have a chance to watch it, odds are there's something wrong with it.

However, in this case, Hussain is right to talk to the audience—because ***Subconscious Cruelty*** is unlike just about anything else out there on the cinematic landscape. If you picked this film up on a lark, solely based on the blurb of the back of the cover, you'd have no idea at all as to what you were in for. Because of this, having Hussain spend a few minutes talking about why he made it and what it means to him is a good thing—it gives the potential unaware viewer one last chance to reach for the escape hatch before the really bad things start happening.

And trust me, really bad things do happen in ***Subconscious Cruelty***—things that would make the Marquis de Sade himself wince. This triptych of perversion and depravity is like a pitbull going for the jugular—and once it gets hold of you, it doesn't let go for the full 80-minute running time. It is a constant barrage of images and sounds designed to both titillate and repulse its audience—many times at the same instance.

The average viewer will undoubtedly compare the movie to the works of David Lynch. I can see where the comparison comes from (anything surreal and not constructed in the typical three-act format tends to be described as "Lynchian" these days), but don't particularly agree with it.

In many ways, I find ***Subconscious Cruelty*** has more in common with the works of Japanese Cyberpunk directors like Shinya Tsukamoto and Shozin Fukui with a touch of inspiration from David Cronenberg also tossed into the mix. The ideas of sexual obsession, bodily mutilation, and twisted religious iconography all seem to tie into the cinematic oeuvres of the aforementioned directors moreso than they do to Lynch's filmography. Add in a dash of Bunuel's work with Salvador Dali and you're on the right track as far as what to expect from the film is concerned.

This isn't to say that ***Subconscious Cruelty*** is a cyberpunk film—because it's not. Nor is it as detached and clinical as the cinema of David Cronenberg (although the first full-length segment, "Human Larvae" does come close). Instead, Hussain has set off for territory all his own—and the journey into these twisted worlds is guaranteed to put off many viewers who don't like their cinema confrontational or graphic.

However, for those of us who don't mind some excellently designed splatter and some thought provoking imagery, there's much to enjoy in the film. It doesn't hit on all cylinders (Hussain was a young man when he made it—it occasionally shows in the dialogue of a piece like "Human Larvae"—what seems pretty profound at 19 is more often pretentious and a little bit trite when one gets closer to 30), but when it works, it's unforgettable.

Perhaps the most striking thing about the film is the way Hussain has managed to seamlessly blend erotic imagery (this film has almost as much full frontal nudity as a porn flick—and even features some hardcore insert shots playing on a television in one segment) and an ever-present feeling of dread. This is particularly true of "Human Larvae" and "Right Brain/Martyrdom" where sexual obsession and perversion lead to some horrific things. The birth scene in "Human Larvae" is gruesome enough, but when one watches the atrocities in "Right Brain/Martyrdom" (which are sure to offend the religious audience members) it's depravity taken to a whole other level.

And that's good news for gorehounds—***Subconscious Cruelty*** certainly delivers the grue and carnage by the veritable bucketload. Highlights include the aforementioned birthing sequence, an icky knife fellating, a cringe-inducing masturbation sequence, Jesus being eaten alive by naked female demons (one of them even urinates on him), and more. Gore fans will certainly get their money's worth out of this package.

Ultimately, though, anyone who only goes in for the gore is missing half the fun ("fun" being a subjective term—there's nothing really fun about this film in the traditional sense of the word). ***Subconscious Cruelty*** is a fever-nightmare of perversion and atrocity captured on celluloid. It has the thematic stylings of Shinya Tsukamoto coupled with the aesthetic lighting and cinematography of men like Mario Bava and Dario Argento. Those looking for a "traditional" gore film are in for a real surprise—this is gore cinema, but it's also proof that gore cinema can be more than shot on camcorder crap appealing to the lowest common denominator. Gore cinema can have a brain and a heart—***Subconscious Cruelty*** proves it

# CHAPTER FORTY-FIVE

# TOKYO GORE POLICE (2009)

**Directed by: Yoshihiro Nishimura**

**Barf Bag Rating:**

TOKYO IS BURNING.
FEVER DREAMS PRESENTS
A TOKYO SHOCK ORIGINAL
STARRING
EIHI SHIINA of AUDITION
a YOSHIHIRO NISHIMURA film
TOKYO
GORE
POLICE

A heady mixture of Takashi Miike's typical Japanese insanity and David Cronenberg's pet theme of bodily dysfunction (with homages to the social parodies of Paul Verhoeven's **Robocop** and **Starship Troopers**), **Tokyo Gore Police** wears its inspirations on its sleeves (right next to all the blood and pieces of flayed flesh...)--it's not a particularly deep film, but if you love Japanese cinema with an abundance of severed limbs, geysering fountains of blood, and cute girls dressed up like they're headed to a cosplay convention, this is a film you'll certainly want to check out.

The hauntingly lovely Eihi Shiina (you may remember her as Asami from Miike's classic, **Audition**) is Ruka. Ruka's a young cop on a special unit designed to hunt down "engineers".

Engineers are some sort of mutants with a weird key-shaped gene that makes them go completely psychotic and murder anyone and everyone in their path. The only way to kill an engineer is to deliver a blow to them that cuts the key in half--any other injury not only doesn't kill them, but instead turns them into Cronenbergian weapons (think the flesh gun from **Videodrome** and you've got it). In this wacky future Japan, the police force has been privatized (which leads to all sorts of room for parody), and when Ruka's not tracking down engineers (or slicing her wrists...) she's seeking to find out who killed her father (a decorated cop assassinated in the line of duty).

The story is the film's greatest shortcoming. **Tokyo Gore Police** runs for a little under two hours, and you often get the feeling that it could have been tightened up significantly. The subplot involving Ruka's father isn't all that interesting (nor is the reveal at the end when she finds the killer) and it eats up some significant screentime in the latter half of the movie. That's the only complaint I have though-the rest of **Tokyo Gore Police** runs like a well-oiled (if that oil were blood...) machine.

**Tokyo Gore Police** succeeds whenever Ruka is required to fight an engineer, and director-slash-special effects wizard Yoshihiro Nishimura understands this implicitly. In the film's early stages, there's some kind of crazy gross gore moment happening roughly every three minutes. Limbs are sliced off, heads removed, eyes plucked, castrations--you name it, it's in here somewhere. Nishimura never forgets that one of the three words of the title is "gore" and as such the film delivers so much carnage and destruction that it's right up there with Jackson's **Dead Alive** and the oeuvre of Olaf Ittenbach when it comes to the most splattery films ever made.

What sets Nishimura's film apart from Ittenbach is that Nishimura seems to be genuinely creative. The gore is thick in **Tokyo Gore Police**, but it's also fairly inventive. There are tons of standard gore gags littered throughout the film (with this much dismemberment, it's a given) but then there are occasions where Nishimura really strives to do something new--take for instance the woman engineer who has the entire lower half of her body turn into crocodile jaws or the guy who develops a giant penis cannon--and the movie manages to surprise you with its inventiveness.

Complementing the grue in **Tokyo Gore Police** is a wacky sense of humor. The film boasts numerous public service advertisements that are genuinely funny and creative. There's a "don't' commit hara-kiri" ad, a great piece on a new Nintendo Wii game that allows the whole family to murder people right from their own living room, and commercials for fashionable wrist-slicers. If that weren't enough, the film boasts a **Battle Royale**-styled Japanese girl who intrudes at various interludes to cheer the police on in their mission to eradicate the engineer plague. All in all, the humor provides a nice counterbalance to all the gory mayhem. This is one of the few gore comedies to get the balance right.

If nothing else, **Tokyo Gore Police** proves that you can make a film that pays homage to other movies yet still maintain an identity of your own while doing it. The title tells you pretty much everything you need to know on this one—if you love quirky Japanese gore flicks, this is well worth your time. It gory and funny and quite possibly one of the best cult films we'll see all year.

# CHAPTER FORTY-SIX

# THE TOXIC AVENGER (1985)

**Directed by: Lloyd Kaufman and Michael Herz**

**Barf Bag Rating:**

Alternate title: *Health Club Horror (1983) (USA: working title)*

He was 98lbs. of solid nerd
until he became...
THE TOXIC AVENGER
A
LLOYD KAUFMAN/
MICHAEL HERZ
PRODUCTION
The first Superhuman-Hero...from New Jersey!
Starring ANDREE MARANDA · MITCHELL COHEN · PAT RYAN, JR · JENNIFER BAPTIST · ROBERT PRICHARD · CINDY MANION · GARY SCHNEIDER · MARK TORGL
Directors of Photography JAMES LONDON and LLOYD KAUFMAN · Original Story by LLOYD KAUFMAN · Written by JOE RITTER · Edited by RICHARD HAINES
Associate Producer STUART STRUTIN · Music Consultant MARC KATZ · Directed by MICHAEL HERZ and LLOYD KAUFMAN
Produced by MICHAEL HERZ and LLOYD KAUFMAN
© TROMA ENTERTAINMENT, INC
DUE TO THE NATURE OF THIS FILM,
NO ONE UNDER 17 WILL BE ADMITTED.

What would you get if you crossed the 1950's style grade Z drive-in monster movie (a la **Creature From the Black Lagoon**) and an '80s style gore flick? You'd probably wind up with something that looks a lot like Lloyd Kaufman and Michael Herz's 1985 cult classic, **The Toxic Avenger**--a movie that's so awful it's great.

Melvin (Mark Torgl) is a 98-pound weakling who works at the Tromaville health club where he's the butt of every joke and even the less fit and attractive ladies don't cast him a second glance. He lives at home with his mom, and spends a large portion of each day mopping the floors of the spa. One day, a practical joke goes a bit too far—causing our nerdy janitor to leap from a second story window after being humiliated in front of a bunch of the club's patrons (keep an eye open for Marisa Tomei as an extra in the health club, by the way).

However, rather than splattering wetly on the sidewalk below, he has the good fortune to land in a vat of toxic waste (the local mayor's more interested in making money by allowing chemical companies dump their waste in Tromaville than in passing and upholding the law). Melvin runs home and undergoes a massive metamorphosis—changing from wimp to muscular (and mutated) crime fighter--and thus **The Toxic Avenger**, the first superhero from New Jersey, is born.

From there, Toxie goes on a one man crusade to clean up the streets of Tromaville—using deadly force to eliminate almost anyone who breaks the law, and even finding time to fall in love with a blind woman named Julie (Andree Maranda) who can't see how awful he really looks.

It's fairly easy (given the film's obviously low budget and schlock film origins) to pick on **The Toxic Avenger**--after all, the performances are almost all over the top, the script and story are nonsensical, and the film's main objective seems to be making the audience laugh at the fact they're repulsed by what's on the screen. But, you could make the argument that this movie is one of the most influential gore comedies to come along in the 1980s (it predates Peter Jackson's **Bad Taste** and Sam Raimi's **Evil Dead 2** by several years—both films that often spring to mind when discussing gory, yet funny, films).

Directors Herz and Kaufman are sort of like Roger Corman—they just want to make movies. Artistic aspirations, awards, and critical acclaim clearly mean very little to these men. Instead, they're governed by a passion to simply tell stories that entertain an audience. There's no sign of the auteur theory at work in any Troma Team production—and frankly, I'm glad there isn't. These guys take every cent they can beg, borrow, or steal and throw it all up on the screen. Sometimes the results are less than stellar, but here, they actually manage to make an entertaining B movie--no small feat considering what they have to work with.

But, trying to discuss a film like ***The Toxic Avenger*** in technical film critic terms is sort of a pointless exercise. This film wasn't made to be scrutinized or dissected—it was made to entertain by appealing to our basest interests: juvenile humor, nudity, and graphic gore—and it's here that the film really succeeds. If you go into a movie like this with your "critic's hat" on, you're bound to come out of it disappointed. Instead, this is a Joe Bob Briggs kind of film—one made to be enjoyed while consuming your favorite alcoholic beverage and hooting at the onscreen carnage.

Speaking of onscreen carnage, the film really delivers here. Toxie knocks off assorted baddies in a variety of creative and interesting ways. Whether it's the by ripping off a guy's arm and beating him with it, deep frying a criminal's hand in a fast food restaurant's fryer, or crushing a guy's head with a set of weights, there are more than enough graphically gory moments to keep even the most jaded gorehounds satisfied in this film.

In the end, I'm a bit biased when it comes to this film. ***The Toxic Avenger*** was one of the first cult gore flicks I ever saw—and it helped inspire my lifelong love of obscure and bizarre movies. My warm and fuzzy feelings aren't just based on nostalgia, though—the film has held up and aged well. Troma has since gone on to become something of a household name in the field of low-budget cult cinema, but ***The Toxic Avenger*** is a great way to see where the House That Lloyd Kaufman Built got its start.

# CHAPTER FORTY-SEVEN

# VIOLENT SHIT (1987)

**Directed by: Andreas Schnaas**

**Barf Bag Rating:**

THE
VIOLENT SHIT
COLLECTION
Synapse
films
DVD
VIDEO

While calling Andreas Schnaas a "filmmaker" feels like something of a stretch, there's no denying that what the man lacks in technical skill is more than compensated for by his love of onscreen carnage. His magnum opus in this arena is his *Violent Shit* series—a multitude of shot-on-video gorefests that make little sense narratively, but pile on the carnage with such over-the-top zeal that you can't help but love them anyway.

1987's *Violent Shit*—which is the first entry in the splatter series—attempts to tell the story of mass murderer Karl the Butcher Shitter (Schnaas). Karl's a madman who's escaped from a police transport van and now kills anyone and everyone he encounters in the most wicked and vile ways imaginable.

The problem with the film is that there's really no rhyme or reason to what's happening onscreen from a narrative perspective. *Violent Shit* features long stretches where no one says much of anything, and a cast of characters who are only introduced so they can be violently dispatched moments later. The film is only tangentially interested in telling a story – functioning instead as a sort of "gag reel" to show off Schnaas' talent for creating gruesome low budget special effects (Schnaas not only directs and stars, he's the lead effects guy too. Quite the Renaissance man).

Despite appearing as though it has a budget made up of all the spare change found in Schnaas' couch, the gore sequences are actually impressive. The film's narrative might be largely nonsensical (is that Jesus who turns up on a cross in front of Karl at one point? If it is, what the hell is he doing in this movie? You'd think the son of God would have a better agent), the gore work really takes things to the next level. There are more geysers of blood in this movie than in the entirety of the Lone Wolf and Cub series—and that's really saying something. Karl the Butcher is nothing if not aptly named.

Describing all of the carnage in *Violent Shit* would leave little time for discussing anything else, so let's just shine a spotlight on a few of the high points.

This film features decapitations, castrations, breast removals, head beatings, a man chopped into pieces by an electric hedge trimmer, and more. The standout sequence is the brutally disgusting vaginal evisceration. It's right up there with the scalpel rape scene in Nacho Cerda's ***Aftermath*** in terms of effectiveness.

Unfortunately, when Karl's not hacking up some hapless German citizen, the movie drags. Most of this is attributable to Schnaas' lack of skill as a director. Since the film has no real plot, any time we shift away from Karl's murder spree, it's readily apparent that Schnaas is simply trying to pad the running time. This is never more apparent than a six-minute sequence featuring a car driving down a road. There's never a payoff—it's just six minutes of uneventful driving.

***Violent Shit***'s other problem is that it was shot on a camcorder—and it shows. Sometimes shot on camcorder films have a certain low-fi charm to them. Here it mostly just looks cheap.

More bothersome, though, is the film's over-reliance on cheap visual effects. I don't mean cheap visual effects like mounting the camera to a shopping cart (which happened in Scott Spiegel's slasher film ***Intruder***), I mean Schnaas' obsession with frame-by-frame slow-mo and blurred footage. Both are used repeatedly in ***Violent Shit***. Neither technique works to the film's advantage.

Despite these myriad flaws, ***Violent Shit*** is included here because it delivers in the one area that really counts: the gore. This is an unrepentantly violent movie, and certainly not for the squeamish. It's also not for those folks who want an actual movie to go along with their heaping helping of splatter, but in this instance I think we can overlook that for the greater good.

# CHAPTER FORTY-EIGHT

# VIOLENT SHIT II (1992)

**Directed by: Andreas Schnaas**

**Barf Bag Rating:**

Alternate title: *Violent Shit 2: Mother Hold My Hand (1992) (USA) (video box title)*

VIOLENT SHIT II
MOTHER HOLD MY HAND
BLOOD PICTURES PRESENTS A REEL GORE PRODUCTION · VIOLENT SHIT II – MOTHER HOLD MY HAND
STARRING ANDREAS DIEHN · ANKE PROTHMANN · ALEXANDER JURKAT MUSIC BY JENS C. MÖLLER
SPECIAL FX BY SVEN PETERSEN · ANDREA POLLAK · WINNI HOLL FX SUPERVISOR ANDREAS SCHNAAS
PHOTOGRAPHED AND EDITED BY STEVE T CHANCE PRODUCTION UNIT FX ASSISTANT MARC TRINKHAUS OPENING TITLE SEQUENCE BY MATTHIAS BECK
EXECUTIVE PRODUCER STEVE AQUILINA PRODUCED BY REEL GORE PRODUCTIONS WRITTEN AND DIRECTED BY ANDREAS SCHNAAS

It may have taken German director Andreas Schnaas five years to make a sequel to ***Violent Shit***, but he finally did it. In those intervening years, it seems as though he spent some time working to improve his craft—which was definitely a good thing. ***Violent Shit II*** won't be winning any technical achievement awards, but gore fans will be pleased to know that it's almost as gruesome as the first installment in the series.

Karl the Butcher Shitter is dead (or is he?), but his son, Karl Jr., is here to continue the killing spree. Karl Jr. (Andreas Schnaas) is a mentally handicapped psychopath living with his mother (Anke Prothmann) in the same woods his father used to haunt. Mom incites Karl Jr. to seek revenge on those who murdered his father, and as such he sets out on a killing spree that would have made Jeffrey Dahmer puke in revulsion. There's also some subplot about a writer working on a story about the murders, but it's essentially nonsensical and serves only a framing device for the main action.

Unlike the first film, which played everything with a deadly seriousness, ***Violent Shit II*** attempts to infuse some comedy into the proceedings. It isn't entirely successful (because watching Karl utter one-liners as he murders his victims seems incredibly forced), but it is far better than the killer's lines in the dreadfully awful ***Nail Gun Massacre***. To be fair, this could be because the film is in German, and the subtitles don't strike me as being particularly well done—I'm sure something could have gotten lost in the translation. However, I think the bigger factor is that this is a low-budget film where Schnaas tried to throw everything he could on the screen whether it actually worked or not—and in the comedy's case, it didn't work at all.

The visuals are still "early generation camcorder", but Schnaas has at least toned down his reliance on the uber-cheesy camera "tricks" he used in the first film. Technically, everything about ***Violent Shit II*** is better than the original—the camera movements more assured, the editing is tighter, and the acting (if you can call it that) is a step up as well.

Yet, despite all of these improvements, ***Violent Shit II*** never manages to be quite as fun or audacious as the original. Karl Jr. actually carries a gun to kill some of his victims this time out—something his dear old dad would have never done. And while there's a pretty nifty (if obviously fake) exploding head sequence, the gun is mainly just used to wing people so that Karl can catch up.

Schnaas has never been a filmmaker afraid of piling on the gore, and this film further cements his reputation as one of splatter cinema's leading practitioners. ***Violent Shit II*** isn't as extreme as the original, but the gore work looks better in a lot of instances, which makes the set-pieces interesting even if they're not as over-the-top as the ones found in the previous film. A highlight of the atrocities on display here includes: a woman having her vagina stapled closed, a woman having her limbs amputated then her skull split in half with a shovel, a testicle hooking, a decapitation followed by oral sex performed with the severed head, and a murder by ruler. I swear, he actually kills someone with a ruler...

Granted, aside from the gore, there's not a whole lot to ***Violent Shit II***—but one gets the impression that Schnaas wasn't exactly aiming to make anything of higher artistic merit than a straight up splatter flick. In this regard, he's successful. While the ***Violent Shit*** films may look like camcorder movies shot in a backyard after a day of binge drinking, they certainly hit the mark when it comes to onscreen carnage.

# Chapter Forty-Nine

# Violent Shit III—Infantry of Doom (1999)

**Directed by: Andreas Schnaas**

**Barf Bag Rating:**

Alternate titles: *VS3: Infantry of Doom (1999) (USA); Violent Shit III (1999) (USA: video box title); Zombie Doom*

THE ARMY OF THE DEAD
SHALL DEVOUR THE LIVING...
ZOMBIE DOOM

Good lord, where to begin...

***Violent Shit III*** is the retitled third installment of low budget German film-maker Andreas Schnaas' ***Violent Shit*** franchise. Like the previous two films, it's high on gore and low on style, yet it's oddly compelling in the same way as gawking at an accident. Taste and decorum tell you to look away, but if you do, you might miss the next really great gory bit.

What little plot the film has can be summed up like this. Three men find themselves on what appears to be a deserted island. However, said island isn't deserted at all—it's the stronghold of Karl the Butcher and Karl Jr. (Andreas Schnaas), maniacal despots who lead an army of iron-masked soldiers against a band of "rebels" that we never see.

Karl and Karl Jr. have been renamed in the DVD version—Karl is Der Meister—I suppose that makes Karl Jr. Der Meister Jr. Why was this done? Probably because having a villain named Karl Jr.(which sounds an awful lot like fast food chain Carl's Jr.) is likely to inspire more laughter than fear...

Anyway, our three leads find themselves guests of Karl—and by being guests, this means that they get to listen to Karl Jr. rant as he executes what seems to be at least half of his own army. One of the three winds up dead, but the other two are released into the surrounding forest to be hunted by Karl's men—sort of a remake of ***The Most Dangerous Game***.

The two heroes (at least we assume they're heroes—they've been the audience's identification point thus far into the film) are joined by an Asian man—an exiled soldier from Karl's army. Said soldier got the boot because he objected to his wife being slaughtered in some kind of fertility experiment that involved some really bad stop motion animation. The fact that the naked European women have some really hairy armpits was far more disturbing to me than any of the gore in the film...

Moving along, our three heroes head into the forest, but rather than run, they decide to stand and fight. Soon, though, they become separated—and the two guys who are still alive from the beginning of the film wind up dead.

The Asian soldier, who's the new lead character by default, meets up with two more Asian guys. Together, they take on a group of ninjas (I swear, I'm not making this up) and destroy Der Meister's base. Of course, our new lead character dies in the process, making the other two Asian guys our last lead characters in the film.

If the overly long plot synopsis serves any purpose, it should demonstrate to you that Andreas Schnaas doesn't have the first clue about narrative structure. The main characters at the end of the film don't even appear until the halfway point, for crying out loud. Factor that in with a script filled with ludicrous dialogue (it's hilariously bad) and absolutely no explanation for why any of these things are happening and you wind up with a bad film.

And yet, despite the flaws, I found myself liking *Violent Shit III* on a number of occasions. It's so awful that it almost becomes sublime in a number of spots. The inclusion of a mad scientist version of Josef Mengele/Adolf Hitler working to build a "Meister Race" is much more clever than what you'd expect to find in a film of this caliber. The whole "Infantry of Doom" thing seems like a send-up of Nazi Germany—at least until you get to the ninjas.

Schnaas is never going to win any awards as a filmmaker, but for a film shot on video (with some artsy inserts utilizing what appears to be 16MM film), *Violent Shit III* is better than a lot of the other crap floating around out there. Schnaas takes particular glee in capturing any gore effect—something this film features in spades.

Much like Olaf Ittenbach's *Premutos*, *Violent Shit III* exists mainly to please gore film fans—one of the few things it does really well. There's no limit to the atrocity that Schnaas films—men are decapitated, shot in the head, blown to bits, have their spinal cords ripped out through their anus and so on. For such a low budget film, the gore work is surprisingly good. If you're a fan of splatter cinema, then *Violent Shit III* is well worth seeing.

*Violent Shit III* is not a good film by conventional standards—and it never pretends to be. The mere fact that it features ninjas, masked madmen, stop motion animation monsters, and loads of kung fu fighting (and, disappointingly, a surprisingly low number of zombies) should make that abundantly clear. Yet, Andreas Schnaas didn't make ***Violent Shit III*** in order to make a "good" film. It's readily apparent that he made it for himself and other gore film fans who don't care much about plot as long as there's lots of really cool effects work. In this regard, Schnaas has succeeded. ***Violent Shit III*** won't appeal to mainstream cinema fans—or even mainstream horror fans—but gore fanatics are going to love it.

# Chapter Fifty

# ZOMBIE (1979)

**Director: Lucio Fulci**

**Barf Bag Rating:**

Alternate titles: *Island of the Flesh-Eaters (1979); Island of the Living Dead (1979); Ultimi zombi, Gli (1979); Zombi 2; Zombie 2: The Dead Are Among Us (1979); Zombie Flesh-Eaters (1979) (UK)*

WE ARE GOING TO EAT YOU!

ZOMBIE
...THE DEAD ARE AMONG US!
Jerry Gross presents "ZOMBIE" starring Tisa Farrow • Ian McCulloch • Richard Johnson • Al Cliver
Story and Screenplay by Elisa Briganti • Produced by Ugo Tucci and Fabrizio De Angelis for Variety Film
Color by Metro Color • Directed by Lucio Fulci • Distributed by The Jerry Gross Organization
There is no explicit sex in this picture.
However, there are scenes of violence which may be considered shocking.
No one under 17 will be admitted.

Released just a few months after George Romero's zombie classic, **Dawn Of The Dead**, Lucio Fulci's **Zombie** was little more than an attempt to cash in on the success of a much better film. Despite this, it still manages to be extremely entertaining, with its over the top gore and campy exploitaition feel making it well worth the price of admission.

The film opens with the Coast Guard intercepting what appears to be an empty sailboat in New York harbor. Ah, but it only *appears* to be empty. On board is a ravenous zombie, who manages to take a nice sized chomp out of the throat of one of the officers before he's riddled with bullets and dumped overboard.

Investigation into the boat's ownership leads to one Ann Bowles (Tisa Farrow, sister of Mia Farrow), the daughter of the boat's owner. Ann is later approached by reporter Peter West (Ian McCulloch), who has discovered a note from her father explaining that he's on some island called Matul, and that he's contracted a strange disease. Ann and Peter decide to travel to Matul and find Ann's father.

Eventually, they do arrive on the island, where they meet Dr. Menard (Richard Johnson). Menard is trying to deal with the island's zombie epidemic by shooting the undead in the head while he searches for a cure. Menard sends our intrepid heroes to check on his wife, Paola (Olga Karlatos). By the time they arrive, Paola is in the process of being zombie lunch, but not before having a gigantic wooden splinter driven through her eye in order to satisfy Fulci's fetish for extreme ocular mayhem. After that, all hell breaks loose as the dead keep rising and our heroes struggle to survive.

**Zombie** is probably Fulci's best known film in the U.S., and while it's a better film than **The Gates Of Hell**, it's not quite on the same level as his masterwork, **The Beyond**. Fulci's direction here is competent, more controlled than his work on **Gates**. There are some of the standard rough edits, the leering shots of gore effects, and some pointless close-ups of characters, but it's not as distracting as it is in some of his earlier efforts.

The film features some great gore effects by Giovani Corridori and Gino de Rossi, notably the aforementioned splinter in the eye. Also worth noting are the zombie attacks and the zombies themselves.

Still, the scene the movie is best known for is relatively gore-less. On the way to Matul, one of the women on the boat decides to go for a dive. While underwater (and topless, no less--you've gotta love the Italians) she encounters a medium sized shark. She also encounters a zombie. What ensues is a battle royale between zombie and fish as each tries to devour the other. The scene adds nothing to the plot, but man, it's a hoot to watch anyway.

Truthfully, ***Zombie*** is little more than an effort by an Italian filmmaker to cash in on the success of ***Dawn Of The Dead***. And while it lacks both the social commentary and the likable characters that made ***Dawn*** such a success, it still manages to work as a fine piece of zombie cinema. Maybe it's the film's utter lack of pretension, or it's obvious low budget origins, but whatever it is, ***Zombie*** is a flick well worth seeking out. Grab this one, call over a few friends, and get ready to be entertained.

# More From The Horror Geek

**Watch Sick Flicks on YouTube**

https://www.youtube.com/c/TheHorrorGeek

**Watch Mike's Grindhouse Gospel on YouTube**

https://www.youtube.com/@GrindhouseGospel

**The Horror Geek on Patreon**

https://www.patreon.com/Horrorgeek

**Coming Soon from Horror Geek Mike Bracken**

**Gore Galore: Sick Flicks Volume II**

**Sympathy for the Devil (a novel)**

# THANKS

What you're holding in your hands is a labor of love and a book that was a very long time coming.

I first got the idea to write Sick Flicks way back in the early 2000s. I was just starting out as a horror and cult film critic, the internet was still relatively new, and not many people were writing about splatter films with any kind of real insight. I saw an opening in the market and I felt like I could fill it.

At the time, ebooks weren't really a thing. Print on demand self publishing was still largely some fantastical vision for the future – and besides, publishing your own book was frowned upon, as anyone who tried to sell a book they paid to publish through a vanity press already knew.

This left one option if I wanted to get Sick Flicks out into the world: traditional publishing.

If you've never tried to sell a book to a publisher before, let me describe it like this – it's a lot like trying to sell ice to eskimos. It's even more challenging when you're a new author trying to sell a non-fiction book on a very niche topic like splatter films...at that point, it's like trying to sell eskimos air conditioners.

Undaunted (and relatively naive), I wrote Sick Flicks and then went out and found a bunch of horror movie books that I liked. I made a list of who published them (it was a short list...) and then I went home and fired off blind unsolicited pitch emails to the publishers convinced that shortly I'd be mired in the middle of a bidding war for the rights to publish my book.

See what I mean about the naive part?

Generally speaking unsolicited, un-agented submissions get trashed or at best wind up in the "slush pile" – a stack of material that the publisher or agent didn't ask for and is not a high priority for them. I suspect that was the fate of a lot of my early queries...

But amazingly enough, either through luck, providence, or simply because I was targeting small publishers and not The Big 5, the pitch for Sick Flicks did actually generate a modest amount of interest.

Academic film book publisher McFarland wrote back, but nothing ever came of it (which was a shame because I love their books and they were my first pick – even though they had tiny print runs and the books were expensive to buy. I was really in it for the prestige...).

While that opportunity was dying on the vine, an editor at Hadesgate reached out to me as well. I'd pitched them because they had done some horror movie books and we're tied in with Gorezone magazine – which felt like a sign from the universe to me.

They expressed interest in Sick Flicks, but instead of wanting to buy it and publish it outright, they told me they had an upcoming book on the greatest slasher movies ever made with essays from a bunch of different filmmakers, jour-nalists, and critics. They had 38 entries, but they wanted an even 40 and wanted to know if I'd be interested in writing two essays for that book as a sort of precursor to them considering taking on Sick Flicks.

I jumped at the opportunity.

I penned two essays for that slasher film book – ones covering Dario Argento's Opera and Michele Soavi's Stagefright – and sent them in. Then, several months later, I got the email every writer dreads: the project was dead.

Except like a slasher film villain, the book came back to life a short time later – albeit with a different publisher and a new title. Darkscribe Press would take on the production duties for the now long out of print *Butcher Knives and Bodycounts*.

After years of delays, that book was finally published – which was great – but Hadesgate was no longer involved and Darkscribe didn't seem particularly interested in publishing my book (and to be fair, at least part of that was because I never really pitched it to them). I was back at square one.

And square one is where this book sat...for years. I had the book edited. I tweaked the line up of reviews. I changed the format multiple times (both lengthening and shortening the final text). But I never sent the book out to publishers again. It was, in the writer's parlance, a "trunk book" – meaning a book you wrote, tried to publish, failed, and then filed away in a trunk with all of your other works that were too ugly to see the light of day.

I would still talk about this mythical book of splatter reviews, and for years people would ask me when it was coming out. I'd just say "I don't know...we're working on it" and then I'd go do something else. If you know me and you're seeing the parallels to the process of selling and publishing my first novel, well, you're not wrong. I'm a hall of famer when it comes to procrastination.

It's been roughly 20 years since I've last sent Sick Flicks out into the world. In that time, I've written a novel (still not published, because I have still not made the edits an agent requested...), written for almost all the major film websites, and most importantly, launched a Youtube channel with a show literally called Sick Flicks.

The publishing game has changed pretty dramatically since the early 2000s too. It's easier than ever to publish a book. Self-publishing through Kindle and the like are no longer viewed like publishing with a vanity press. You don't have to have an agent anymore and you don't have to publish through the Big 5 (or Big 3 or whatever they've cannibalized themselves into these days). In fact, with declining marketing budgets and paltry advances, there's a case to be made that it's actually better to publish your own work if you have an audience and platform. You control your own creative output – which is amazing.

It was this epiphany, coupled with the success of my Youtube channel, that finally made me realize it was time to publish Sick Flicks. It's been 20 years since I first started writing this thing (even longer if you add in the years I spent as a kid watching all these films and learning about them and all that) – which feels like a lifetime. During that stretch I've been on TV, gotten married, gotten divorced, moved cross country, been so broke I couldn't afford food, grew dreadlocks and chopped them off (HUGE mistake), became a powerlifter, wrote a novel, launched a Youtube channel, lost too many friends and my grandparents to Father Time, watched a LOT of movies, and met my dream girl. Having Sick Flicks sitting in a trunk felt like unfinished business...so consider this me finishing it.

Except, this is also a beginning. There are more gore flicks out there than are covered in this book. Sick Flicks the book was never intended to be a single volume – it's a series of books. Which means I now need to wrap this up and get to work on Sick Flicks Volume 2: More Gore!

I hope you'll join me for that one and the ones that come after it. I hope you'll check out my novel when it finally gets finished. I hope you'll continue to check out my Youtube channel. But mostly I hope you enjoy the book and that it helps you discover new movies to add to your watch list or lets you look at old favorites in a new light.

## Acknowledgements

Writing a book is a largely solitary process. You sit alone, quietly, at a keyboard and funnel words onto a screen until the thing is done. Making Youtube videos is not a whole lot different (except you spend your day writing, then talking to a camera in an empty room).

And yet, no creative project is brought to fruition without the help, guidance, and inspiration of others. This book is no exception. As such, I'd like to thank the following people for their love and guidance throughout my career. There are too many of you to hit everyone, so my apologies if I missed you. The acknowledgements and afterword of this book could be longer the main text at this point....

My dear friend Constantin Preda. I've known Con since high school – and I've watched him carve out a career in film and television production that inspires me to this day. Easily the most outgoing, gregarious, kind-hearted person I know...and man, could he dance.

I've wanted to be a writer since I was in kindergarten. In fourth grade, I was fully into it, creating my first comic – the adventures of a superhero duck (imaginatively named Super Duck) and his rogue's gallery of villains. Mrs. Hatcher, my fourth grade teacher, let me read each day's new Super Duck adventure to the class and it was the first time I saw the power of being a storyteller. Seeing my friends react to each new story was intoxicating. I'm sure Mrs. Hatcher is no longer with us, but without her the road of my life might have been very different.

The same can be said of my friend Sean Sexton. Sean was my sophomore year English teacher (and has probably died a dozen deaths at all the terrible mistakes I've made in this book...) and then my creative writing teacher senior year. Sean convinced me that this writing thing was a doable career (I doubt I'd have been dissuaded anyway). He made me a better writer, but he also made me a better thinker (which was important in terms of being a critic). Any of the things I do well writing-wise are attributable to his guidance. The mistakes are my own, so don't blame him.

Next up, this book wouldn't exist without the guidance and friendship of film critic Walter Chaw. I've known Walter for like 20 years now and he remains one of the most insightful, intelligent, and persuasive critics in the biz, but also one of my favorite people (which is a big thing because I am a hardcore misanthrope at heart). I aspire to be even half as good at this thing as he is. He regularly makes me look at films in new ways, which is a real gift in the current film criticism world where everything is aggregated, homogenized, and well....bland. Walter is a true original – and I love him for that.

Finally, I can't not mention my significant other, Lisa Daily. Without Lisa, I'm almost certain I'd have never gotten this book off the ground and across the finish line. I'm 100% positive I'd have never written a novel. Where I'm a procrastinator and a dreamer and often paralyzed by a fear of failure, she is the opposite. Whenever I need a push, she's there – breaking down giant fear-inspiring projects into manageable chunks, giving me pep talks, or just telling me to stop fretting about things that haven't happened yet. She's the unstoppable force of optimism to my immovable object of worst case scenarios. I love her for that.

All right, we gotta move this along....

A big thanks to my parents for creating me. You probably deserve a medal for that...and a medal for enduring me. Love you, guys.

More love to my daughter Jasmine, my grandson Sterling, and my stepkids Monica, Gabe, Quinn, and Elle. You guys keep me young, while also making me feel very old.

Can't forget my nieces and nephews, Madison, Aiden (aka Steve), Olivia (aka Ia) and Landon (aka Lando). You guys did pretty well in the cool uncle department...

Keeping with the family vibe, lots of love to Grannie Janny. She doesn't like gross movies, but she watched Sick Flicks every week in the early days just to be supportive.

Huge shoutout to Ryan Harding. Ryan is the king of grossout fiction. We first met way back in the mid 90s on the Horrornet message boards and have been friends ever since. We share a love of gross shit, questionable movies, extreme fiction, and worst case scenarios. Ryan was instrumental early on in finding some of these films before the DVD era.

Keeping on that path, thanks to the entire Horrornet cabal. Feo Amante (who gave me my first gig writing reviews), Brian Keene, Brian Hodge, Ed Lee, Coop, Mikey, Mike Oliveri, Regina Mitchell, and those we've lost like Richard Laymon, Jack Ketchum, John Pelan, JF Gonzalez, and Tom Piccirilli. I learned so many invaluable lessons about the biz and writing in general from you guys. I can only hope to pay that forward.

I'd be remiss not to mention the inimitable Joe Bob Briggs. I found Joe Bob way back in the Drive-In Theater Days. We did not have The Movie Channel, so I'd stay up late and fiddle with the dial on my cable box like a thief trying to crack a safe to find that perfect spot where the scrambled picture became relatively clear just to see what Joe Bob was covering that week. Joe Bob not only helped broaden my love of cult cinema, he showed me you could make a career out of talking about it.

By that same token, I have to thank the Best Brains/Mystery Science Theater/Rifftrax crew. I've never made any bones about the fact that Sick Flicks on

Youtube is little more than a poor man's MST3K ripoff, but it wouldn't exist without the work of guys like Mike, Joel, Trace, Frank, Bill, Kevin, and Mary Jo. Seeing MST3K for the first time was like the most life-altering thing ever – guys making obscure pop culture references to B-movies? It's like they knew me... I can't pay you royalties (please don't sue me...), but drinks are on me if ever we meet up.

Keeping things rolling, I have to give a huge thank you to Danny aka Geekdom101. I've known Danny for years and he's the guy who came to me back in 2018 and said "man, I'm killing it on Youtube...you need to be over here making videos." Without that conversation, The Horror Geek channel wouldn't exist. When I have questions or thoughts about video strategy, he's always got insights. Thanks for that.

This is getting really long and there are so many people left...who knew this was going to be such a challenge?

Big thanks to my creative friends Chris Bickel (filmmaker extraordinaire – I fully suspect we'll be covering his films in a book one of these days), Jonathan Doe of Cinema's Underbelly (ditto on the movies thing), my pal Jeremiah Kipp (I know a lot of talented filmmakers...), Donlee Brussell (ANOTHER filmmaker...), Paul Salamoff (another talented filmmaker who can also proudly claim he beat The Horror Geek in a final round showdown on Beat the Geeks), Travis Lowell, John Nesbit, and Laurie Edwards, writer pals Joe Clifford, the amazing Stephen Graham Jones, Scott Weinberg, and Nicholas Kaufmann.

Oh, can't forget my other horror Youtubers too – Brandon Tenold, James "Dead Meat" Janisse, The Cinema Snob, Decker Shado, Stitched Together Pictures, Spooky Rice, and Jay Bond of Bloodbath and Beyond/BTV/Jay Bond Reacts. You guys inspire me to keep getting better.

Finally, thanks to you – the reader – and my audience of Gore Geeks on Youtube. Going on Youtube can be a really humbling experience. They tell new creators not to read the comments because they're often full of demoralizing and revolting things – but my audience is amazing. You guys come to premieres, you buy merch, you support the show with comments, views, and patreon pledges. You share the videos and come to conventions and I can't thank you enough for that. I do this shit for you guys.

9 781969 393013